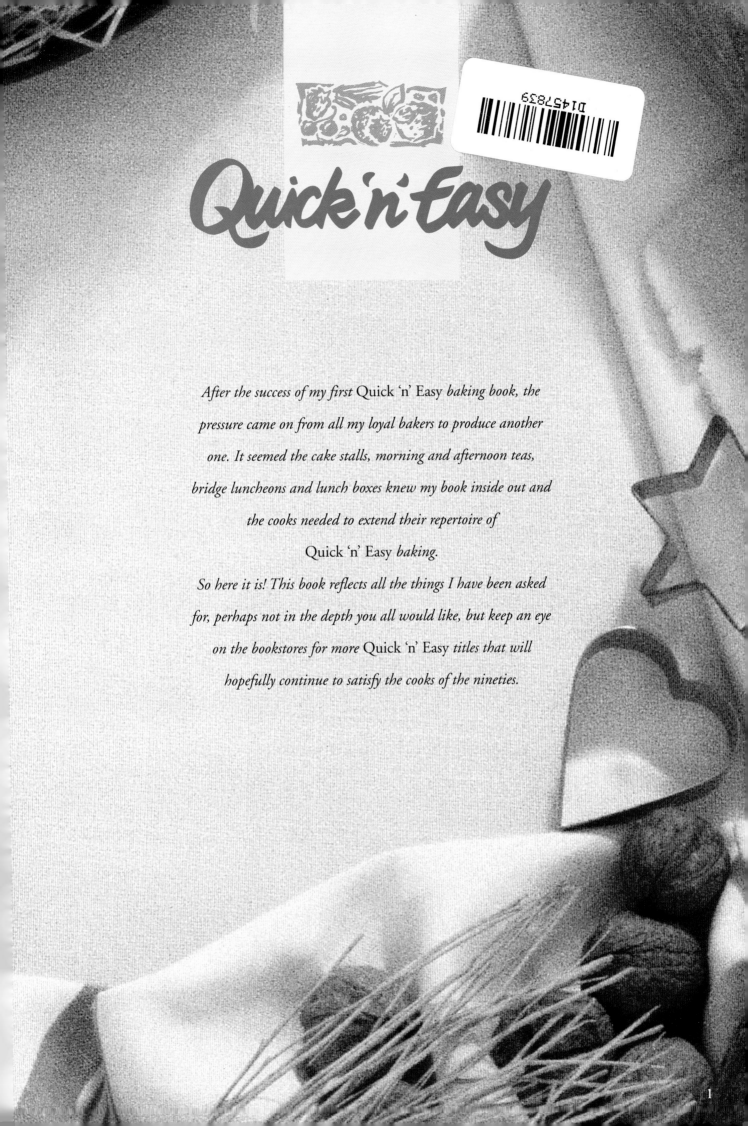

Quick 'n' Easy

After the success of my first Quick 'n' Easy baking book, the

pressure came on from all my loyal bakers to produce another

one. It seemed the cake stalls, morning and afternoon teas,

bridge luncheons and lunch boxes knew my book inside out and

the cooks needed to extend their repertoire of

Quick 'n' Easy *baking.*

So here it is! This book reflects all the things I have been asked

for, perhaps not in the depth you all would like, but keep an eye

on the bookstores for more Quick 'n' Easy *titles that will*

hopefully continue to satisfy the cooks of the nineties.

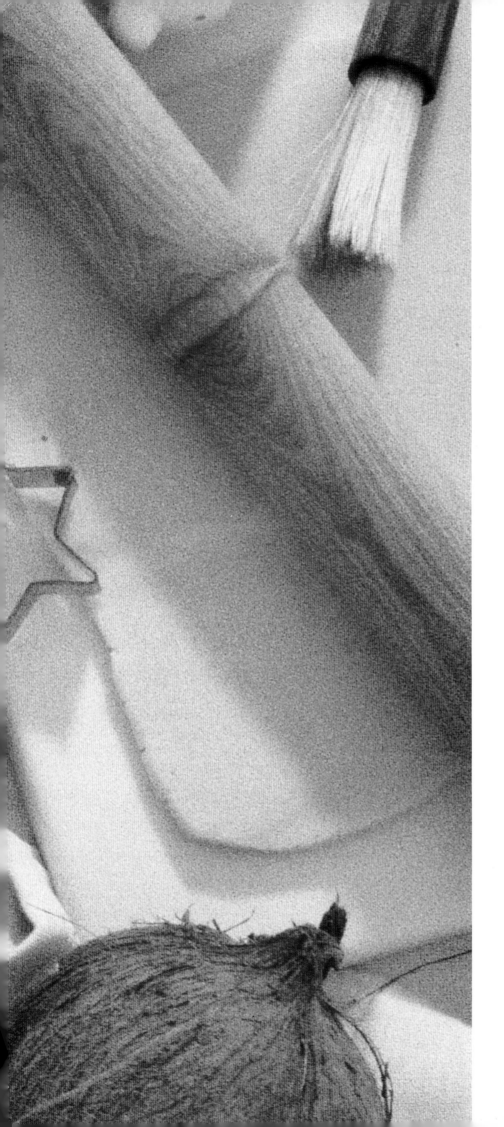

ISBN 1-877193-35-6

© Design & Illustrations –
Concept Publishing
© Text – Robyn Martin

First published in 1995 by
Hodder Moa Beckett Publishers Limited
Reprinted in 1998 by
Concept Publishing
Fax 64-9-489 5335

Photography by
Alan Gillard

Recipe Testing by Robyn Martin,
Jo Blackman, Linda Laycock,
Alison Sherning

Slipcast Earthenware by
Catherine Anselmi, Broadway,
Newmarket, Auckland

Children's Teaset from Russells,
High Street, Auckland

Layout & Type Imaging by
Hot House Design Group Limited

Printed in Hong Kong by
Bookprint International Limited

All recipes in this book have been tested
using New Zealand standard measuring
cups and spoons. All cup and spoon
measures are level and brown sugar
measures are firmly packed.
Standard No. 6 eggs are used.

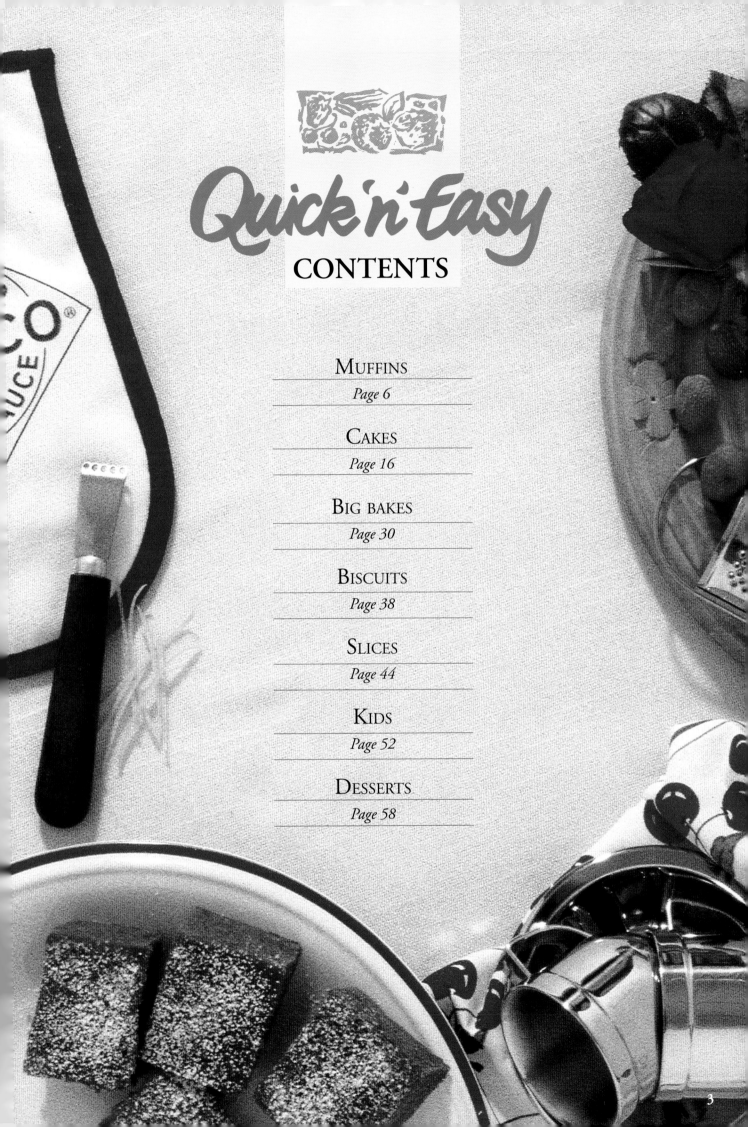

Quick 'n' Easy
CONTENTS

CHELSEA SUGAR

Chelsea Sugar has been a household name in New Zealand for over 110 years, providing a wide range of quality sugar products to the household and the food industry.

The Chelsea Sugar Refinery on the shores of the Waitemata Harbour in Birkenhead, Auckland, has been producing sugar since 1884.

All sugars produced at Chelsea are made from sugar cane. No alternative ingredient can match the positive and varied characteristics of sugar. As a member of the carbohydrate family, sugar is a natural source of energy. Taken in moderation, sugar, and foods containing sugar, provide interest and enjoyment to a well-balanced and healthy diet.

Acting as a natural preservative, sugar maintains the texture and original colours of jams or bottled fruit. It also adds to the keeping quality and texture of cakes and biscuits and assists with the setting of jams or jellies. For bread and buns, sugar is necessary for yeast to grow, to give flavour to the crust and to retain moisture so the bread stays fresh. Sugar provides sweetness and body to beverages and acts as a flavour enhancer in many different foods.

Chelsea is pleased to be associated with this series of Quick 'n' Easy recipe books. We hope you enjoy trying these delicious recipes using our Chelsea Sugars!

For more recipes or information write to:
New Zealand Sugar Ltd, Freepost 1188, PO Box 30, Auckland 1.

CHELSEA SUGARS AND THEIR USES
Raw Sugar
This natural granulated sugar is used as a sweetener for coffee, or in baking and cooking, where it improves the flavour and colour of the end result.

Demerara
Harvested from the canefields of Mauritius, Demerara is one of the finest sugars to enhance the flavour of coffee. The fine syrup coating on the crystals adds a distinctive molasses flavour and the coarseness of crystal gives a good colour to the crust of baking.

White Sugar

Here's one we all know and love! The uniform size of the sugar crystals gives you a regular texture and consistency, making it the perfect ingredient for baking and sweets. It does not have colour or flavour and will therefore enhance food flavours, not disguise them.

Caster Sugar

Caster sugar dissolves easily so it is ideal for meringues, puddings, jellies and cake mixes. When used in baking, caster sugar, with its smaller sugar crystals, caramelises evenly so it produces a fine golden colour in the finished product.

Icing Sugar

While no cake would be complete without it, icing sugar can also be used to make goodies such as shortbread, cream fillings, marshmallow and fondant, anywhere a smooth, soft-finished texture is required.

Soft Brown Sugar

This popular sugar is used in many recipes, both savoury and sweet. A concentration of natural syrups gives it the dark colour and rich flavour. Its unique flavour makes it suitable for caramels, toppings and sauces.

Coffee Crystals

As the name suggests, this sugar is the perfect sweetener for coffee (or any other hot drink for that matter!). The large-sized crystals are coated with a thin layer of syrup, which provides a unique caramel flavour. Coffee Crystals can also be used in crumble topping for desserts and cakes, and as an attractive topping on biscuits.

Golden Syrup

Made to the traditional recipe available only in New Zealand and Australia, Chelsea Golden Syrup is the perfect baking ingredient for adding moisture, colour and flavour. Gingernuts, Brandy Snaps and Anzac Biscuits are just a few examples of how Golden Syrup can be used to produce a deliciously rich, chewy result. Available in 1kg tin or 500g easy pour bottle.

Treacle

Ideal for creating moist, flavoursome cakes and biscuits. Treacle has a richer colour than Golden Syrup and a stronger, slightly bitter flavour.

Quick 'n' Easy

MUFFINS

It is hard to imagine that anyone could come up with an
original muffin recipe with a flavour combination that hasn't
been tried already.

There are a few favourites in this chapter that I have no doubt
have been done before, but some ideas for muffins are out of my
head. They show how versatile a simple muffin mixture can be.

Vary the size of your muffins depending on the occasion you
plan to serve them.

Mini muffins make an excellent goodie to serve with drinks,
or a jumbo muffin can be a grand start to the day when served
for a weekend breakfast.

ORANGE SUGAR CUBE MUFFINS

2 cups flour
4 teaspoons baking powder
1/4 cup Chelsea Sugar
100g butter
2 teaspoons grated orange rind
2 eggs
1 cup orange juice
Chelsea Sugar Cubes

Sift flour and baking powder into a bowl. Mix in sugar. Make a well in the centre of the dry ingredients. Melt the butter. Beat orange rind, eggs and orange juice together until combined. Pour into dry ingredients and mix to just moisten. Three-quarter fill greased, deep muffin tins. Rub each sugar cube over the grated surface of the orange used for the orange rind. Place a sugar cube in the centre of each muffin. Bake at 190°C for 20 minutes or until muffins spring back when lightly touched.

Makes about 12.

LEMON YOGHURT MUFFINS

2 cups flour
3 teaspoons baking powder
1/4 cup Chelsea Sugar
50g butter
2 eggs
1 teaspoon grated lemon rind
1/4 cup lemon juice
1 cup natural unsweetened yoghurt

Sift flour and baking powder into a bowl. Mix in sugar. Make a well in the centre of the dry ingredients. Melt butter. Beat eggs, lemon rind, juice and yoghurt together until combined. Pour butter and egg mixture into dry ingredients and mix to just moisten. Three-quarter fill greased, deep muffin tins. Bake at 200°C for 15 minutes or until muffins spring back when lightly touched.

Makes about 12.

Orange Sugar Cube Muffins and Lemon Yoghurt Muffins

7

Quick'n'Easy

CHOCOLATE CHERRY MUFFINS

1¹/₂ cups flour

¹/₄ cup cocoa

3 teaspoons baking powder

¹/₂ cup Chelsea Soft Brown Sugar

100g butter

2 eggs

³/₄ cup milk

³/₄ cup halved glacé cherries

Sift flour, cocoa and baking powder into a bowl. Stir in brown sugar. Make a well in the centre of the dry ingredients. Melt butter. Beat eggs and milk together. Pour butter, milk mixture and cherries into dry ingredients. Mix to just moisten. Three-quarter fill greased, deep muffin tins. Bake at 190°C for 20 minutes or until muffins spring back when lightly touched.

Makes 10.

LIME MARMALADE MUFFINS

Use any marmalade for this recipe but lime has a wonderful flavour. These make a great breakfast treat.

2 cups flour

4 teaspoons baking powder

¹/₄ cup Chelsea Sugar

¹/₂ cup lime marmalade

2 eggs

1 cup milk

50g butter

Sift flour and baking powder into a bowl. Stir in sugar. Make a well in the centre of the dry ingredients. Beat marmalade, eggs and milk together. Melt butter. Pour milk mixture and butter into dry ingredients. Mix to just moisten. Three-quarter fill greased, deep muffin tins or jumbo muffin tins. Bake at 200°C for 15 minutes for regular muffins or 20 minutes for jumbo muffins.

Makes about 10 regular muffins, or 6 jumbo muffins.

CHOCOLATE SURPRISE MUFFINS

I used this muffin idea in an Easter feature in the *New Zealand Woman's Weekly*. It worked so well it seems a pity to leave it to a back issue of the *Weekly* so here's a deliciously sinful muffin for Easter eating.

2¹/₂ cups flour

4 teaspoons baking powder

¹/₄ cup cocoa

1 teaspoon cinnamon

100g butter

1 cup Chelsea Soft Brown Sugar

1¹/₂ cups milk

1 egg

100g cooking chocolate

15 very small caramel or hazelnut filled Easter eggs

Sift flour, baking powder, cocoa and cinnamon into a bowl. Cut butter through until crumb-like. Stir in the brown sugar. Beat milk and egg together. Melt the chocolate over hot water. Add milk mixture and melted chocolate to the dry ingredients. Mix to just moisten. Spoon about two tablespoons of the mixture into well-greased, deep muffin tins. Unwrap the Easter eggs and place one in the centre of each muffin mixture. Cover evenly with remaining batter. Bake at 180°C for 10 to 15 minutes or until muffins spring back when lightly touched. Serve warm or cold.

Makes 15.

Chocolate Surprise Muffins, Chocolate Cherry Muffins and Lime Marmalade Muffins

PEAR AND GINGER MUFFINS

This is a good way to use up a few pear slices you may have left over from something else. Crystallised ginger makes a good alternative to pears.

2¹/₂ cups flour
2 teaspoons baking powder
2 teaspoons ground ginger
1 teaspoon cinnamon
100g butter
¹/₂ cup Chelsea Sugar
¹/₄ cup Chelsea Golden Syrup
2 eggs
2 teaspoons baking soda
1 cup milk
4 cooked pear quarters

Sift flour, baking powder, ginger and cinnamon into a bowl. Melt butter and mix in sugar, golden syrup and eggs. Beat with a rotary beater until frothy. Dissolve baking soda in milk. Make a well in the centre of the dry ingredients. Add butter and milk mixtures. Mix to just moisten. Three-quarter fill greased, deep muffin tins. Wipe pears with a paper towel. Cut into slices and arrange two to three slices on top of each muffin. Bake at 190°C for 20 minutes or until muffins spring back when lightly touched.

Makes about 12.

Pear and Ginger Muffins, Chilli Whammy Muffins and Cheesy Bran Muffins

CHEESY BRAN MUFFINS

Savoury muffins are very popular. Try cooking two favourite muffin flavours with this delicious cheese and bran combination.

1 cup flour
2 teaspoons baking powder
1¹/₂ cups baking bran
1 cup grated tasty cheese
1 egg
1¹/₄ cups milk

Sift flour and baking powder into a bowl. Mix in bran and cheese. Make a well in the centre of the dry ingredients. Beat egg and milk together and add to dry ingredients. Mix to just moisten. Three-quarter fill greased, deep muffin tins. Bake at 200°C for 15 minutes or until muffins spring back when lightly touched.

Makes 8.

CHILLI WHAMMY MUFFINS

¹/₂ x 125g block cream cheese
2 cups flour
4 teaspoons baking powder
50g butter
2 eggs
1 cup milk
2 to 3 teaspoons Tabasco sauce
2 tablespoons sesame seeds

Cut cream cheese into 1cm cubes. Sift flour and baking powder into a bowl. Make a well in the centre of the dry ingredients. Melt butter. Beat eggs, milk and Tabasco sauce together until combined. Pour egg mixture and butter into dry ingredients. Mix to just combine. Half fill greased, deep muffin tins. Place a cube of cream cheese in the centre of each muffin. Top with muffin mixture to three-quarter fill tins. Sprinkle with sesame seeds. Bake at 200°C for 15 minutes or until muffins spring back when lightly touched.

Makes about 10.

11

Quick 'n' Easy

OLIVE AND FETTA MUFFINS

2 cups flour

3 teaspoons baking powder

50g butter

1 egg

100g fetta cheese

1 cup milk

1 cup chopped pitted black olives

1 teaspoon rosemary

Sift flour and baking powder into a bowl. Make a well in the centre of the dry ingredients. Melt butter. Beat in egg. Cut cheese into 1cm cubes. Add butter mixture, milk, cheese, olives and rosemary to dry ingredients. Mix to just moisten. Three-quarter fill greased, deep mini muffin tins or regular deep muffin tins. Bake at 190°C for 10 to 15 minutes for mini muffins or 20 to 25 minutes for regular sized muffins. Serve warm, filled with cheese or pastrami.

Makes 30 mini muffins, or about 12 regular muffins.

PESTO AND PASTRAMI MUFFINS

Pesto can be bought ready-made from the supermarket. If you are not into pesto, substitute it with olive oil and chopped basil. Any cooked flavoursome meat can be used instead of pastrami.

6 slices pastrami

2 cups flour

4 teaspoons baking powder

1/4 cup pesto

2 eggs

1 1/4 cups milk

Cut pastrami into thin pieces. Sift flour and baking powder into a bowl. Make a well in the centre of the dry ingredients. Beat pesto, eggs and milk together until combined. Pour into dry ingredients. Add pastrami and mix until dry ingredients are just moistened. Three-quarter fill deep, greased muffin tins. Bake at 190°C for 20 minutes or until muffins spring back when lightly touched.

Makes about 10.

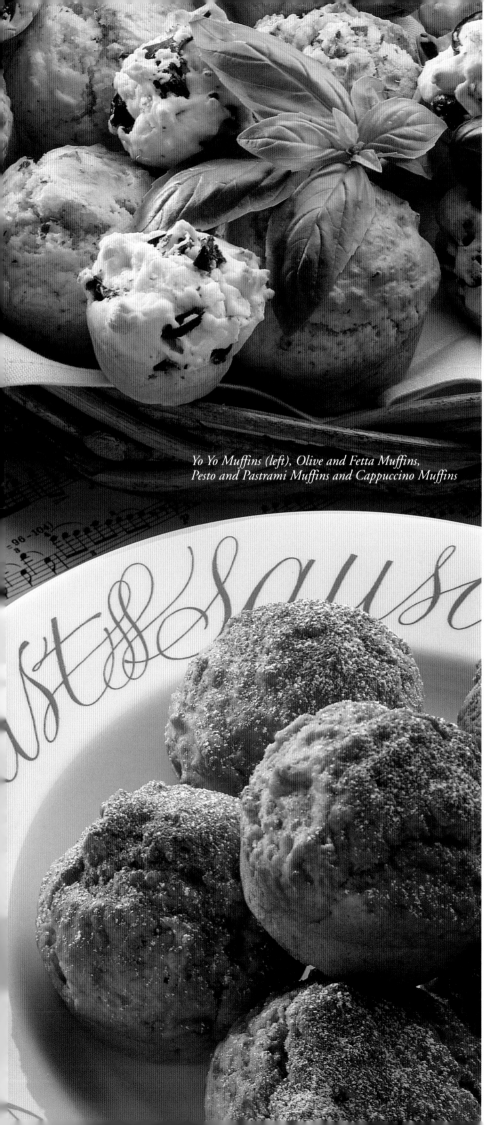

Yo Yo Muffins (left), Olive and Fetta Muffins,
Pesto and Pastrami Muffins and Cappuccino Muffins

CAPPUCCINO MUFFINS

Use leftover coffee for this recipe.
Mini muffins are an ideal size for a
morning tea when other foods are
being served.

2 cups flour
3 teaspoons baking powder
1/2 cup Chelsea Soft Brown Sugar
1/4 cup cream
1 egg
1 cup cold very strong black coffee
Chelsea Icing Sugar

Sift flour and baking powder into a
bowl. Mix in brown sugar. Make a well
in the centre of the dry ingredients.
Beat cream and egg together until
combined. Pour into dry ingredients
with coffee. Mix to just moisten.
Three-quarter fill greased, deep mini
muffin tins or regular greased, deep
muffin tins. Bake at 190°C for 10 to
15 minutes for mini muffins or 15 to
20 minutes for regular muffins, or
until muffins spring back when lightly
touched. Dust with sifted icing sugar
to serve.

*Makes 24 mini muffins, or about 10
regular muffins.*

YO YO MUFFINS

1 1/2 cups flour
1/2 cup custard powder
3 teaspoons baking powder
1/4 cup Chelsea Sugar
100g butter
2 eggs
1 cup milk
1/4 cup raspberry jam

Sift flour, custard powder and baking
powder into a bowl. Mix in sugar.
Make a well in the centre of the dry
ingredients. Melt butter. Beat eggs and
milk together. Add butter and milk
mixture to dry ingredients. Mix to just
moisten. Half fill greased, deep muffin
tins with the mixture. Place a teaspoon
of jam on the mixture in the tin. Top
with more muffin mixture to three-
quarter fill tins. Bake at 190°C for 15
minutes or until muffins spring back
when lightly touched.

Makes about 10.

13

TOMATO AND BASIL MUFFINS

Sundried tomatoes are extremely popular at the moment. For my money they are grossly overrated and much too expensive. However, if you're a fan here's a muffin recipe.

2 cups flour
3 teaspoons baking powder
½ teaspoon salt
1 teaspoon Chelsea Sugar
3 tablespoons oil from the sundried tomatoes
2 eggs
1 cup milk
2 tablespoons chopped fresh basil
¼ cup drained sundried tomatoes in oil

Sift flour, baking powder and salt into a bowl. Stir in sugar. Make a well in the centre of the dry ingredients. Beat the oil, eggs and milk together until combined. Pour into the dry ingredients. Add the basil and sundried tomatoes. Mix to just moisten. Three-quarter fill greased, deep mini muffin tins or regular deep muffin tins. Bake at 190°C for 10 to 15 minutes for mini muffins, 20 minutes for regular muffins or until muffins spring back when lightly touched.

Makes 30 mini muffins, or about 12 regular muffins.

Apricot Muffins (left), Tomato and Basil Muffins and Walnut and Blue Cheese Muffins

WALNUT AND BLUE CHEESE MUFFINS

100g wedge blue vein cheese
½ cup chopped walnuts
2 cups flour
4 teaspoons baking powder
1 tablespoon Chelsea Sugar
2 eggs
1 cup milk
Fresh pear slices

Crumble blue vein cheese into a bowl large enough to mix muffins in. Add walnuts and mix. Sift flour and baking powder into the bowl. Stir in sugar. Make a well in the centre of the dry ingredients. Beat eggs and milk together. Pour into dry ingredients. Mix to just moisten. Three-quarter fill deep, greased mini muffins tins or regular deep muffin tins. Bake at 190°C for 10 to 15 minutes for mini muffins, 20 minutes for regular muffins or until muffins spring back when lightly touched. Serve with sliced fresh pear.

Makes 30 mini muffins, or about 12 regular muffins.

APRICOT MUFFINS

½ cup chopped dried apricots
½ cup water
100g butter
½ cup Chelsea Soft Brown Sugar
1 egg
½ cup milk
2 cups flour
4 teaspoons baking powder

Place apricots and water in a saucepan large enough to mix all the ingredients. Bring to the boil and cook for 5 minutes. Remove from heat. Stir in butter and brown sugar and mix until butter melts. Beat egg and milk together and add to saucepan. Mix well. Sift flour and baking powder into saucepan and mix to just moisten. Three-quarter fill greased, deep muffin tins. Bake at 190°C for 15 to 20 minutes or until muffins spring back when lightly touched.

Makes about 10.

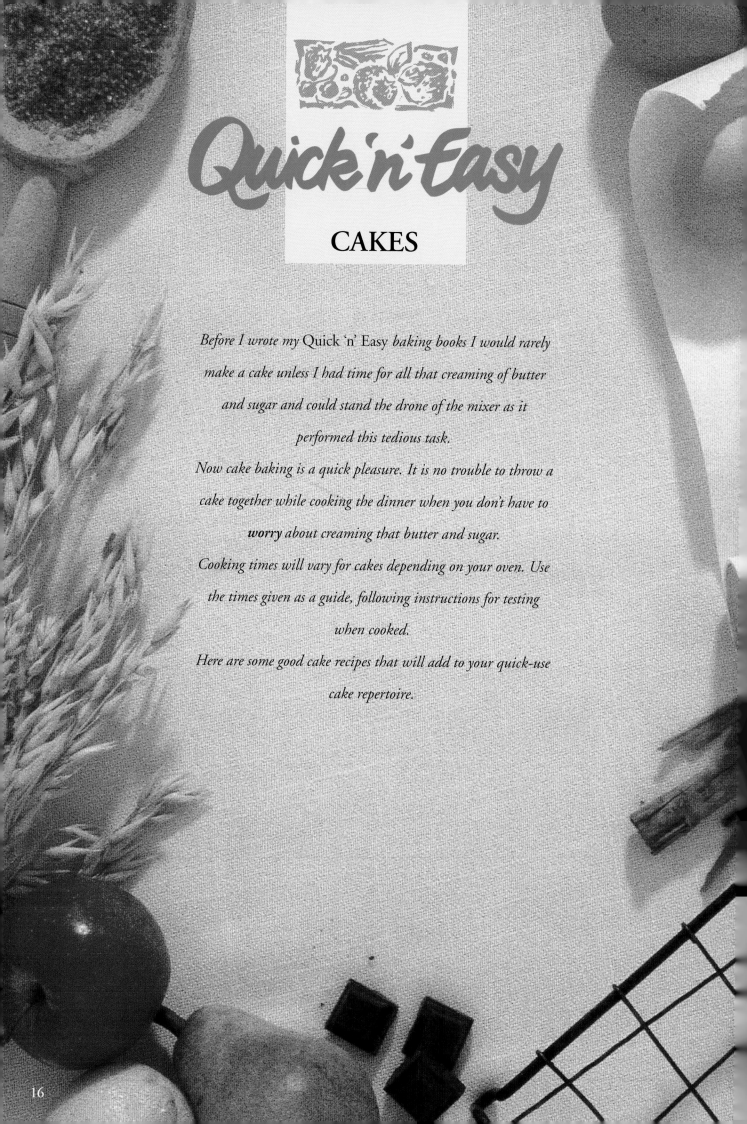

Quick 'n' Easy

CAKES

Before I wrote my Quick 'n' Easy *baking books I would rarely make a cake unless I had time for all that creaming of butter and sugar and could stand the drone of the mixer as it performed this tedious task.*

Now cake baking is a quick pleasure. It is no trouble to throw a cake together while cooking the dinner when you don't have to **worry** *about creaming that butter and sugar.*

Cooking times will vary for cakes depending on your oven. Use the times given as a guide, following instructions for testing when cooked.

Here are some good cake recipes that will add to your quick-use cake repertoire.

MACAROON CAKE

I can remember making a cake like this when I was first allowed to bake. The recipe was in one of the many leaflets I sent away for and it was a cake that was always enjoyed. Here's a quick version for the 1990s. This cake uses the egg yolks in the cake and the egg whites in the topping.

100g butter

½ cup Chelsea Sugar

3 egg yolks

1½ cups flour

2 teaspoons baking powder

½ cup milk

1 teaspoon vanilla essence

½ cup raspberry jam

TOPPING

3 egg whites

¾ cup Chelsea Sugar

1½ cups coconut

1 teaspoon almond essence

Melt butter in a saucepan large enough to mix all the ingredients. Stir in sugar and egg yolks. Sift flour and baking powder into the saucepan. Add milk and vanilla essence and mix with a wooden spoon to combine. Spread mixture into a baking paper-lined 20cm ring tin. A springform pan or loose-bottom cake tin is best. Spread jam over batter. Spread topping over. Bake at 180°C for 45 to 50 minutes or until an inserted skewer comes out clean. Cool in tin for 10 minutes before quickly inverting onto a clean teatowel-covered cooling rack, then turning onto another rack so topping does not get broken.

TOPPING

Beat egg whites until stiff. Gradually beat in sugar and continue beating until mixture is thick. Mix in coconut and almond essence.

Macaroon Cake

17

BOWLS CAKE

Tennis has a cake named after it so I think bowls should have one too!

150g butter
1/2 cup Chelsea Soft Brown Sugar
2 tablespoons marmalade
1 cup raisins
1 teaspoon vanilla essence
1 cup hot water
2 eggs
1 cup flour
1 cup wholemeal flour
4 teaspoons baking powder

Place butter, brown sugar, marmalade, raisins, vanilla essence and water in a saucepan large enough to mix all the ingredients. Bring to the boil. Remove from heat and cool. Using a wooden spoon, beat in eggs, flours and baking powder. Pour mixture into a baking paper-lined 22cm loaf tin. Bake at 180°C for 45 to 50 minutes or until an inserted skewer comes out clean. Leave in tin for 10 minutes before turning onto a cooling rack.

HONEY CAKE

Measure honey in a measuring cup rather than a measuring jug for this recipe.

150g butter
1/2 cup Chelsea Soft Brown Sugar
1/2 cup honey
2 eggs
2 cups flour
3 teaspoons baking powder
1 teaspoon vanilla essence
Chelsea Icing Sugar

Place the butter, brown sugar and honey in a saucepan large enough to mix all the ingredients. Heat, stirring until butter melts. Remove from heat and cool slightly before beating in eggs, flour, baking powder and vanilla essence until mixture is combined. Pour into a baking paper-lined 20cm round cake tin. Bake at 180°C for 45 to 50 minutes or until cake springs back when lightly touched. Leave in tin for 10 minutes before turning out onto a cooling rack. Dust with sifted icing sugar.

CHOCOLATE CAKE

Many chocolate cakes have a disappointing flavour. Try this one for a good chocolate taste.

1/4 cup cocoa
1/4 cup hot water
125g butter
3/4 cup Chelsea Sugar
3 eggs
1 1/2 cups flour
3 teaspoons baking powder
1/2 teaspoon Chelsea Icing Sugar
1/4 teaspoon cocoa

Place first measure of cocoa, water and butter in a saucepan large enough to mix all the ingredients. Heat until butter has melted and cocoa blended. Remove from heat and mix in sugar and eggs, beating until combined. Mix in sifted flour and baking powder until combined. Pour into a baking paper-lined 20cm square cake tin. Bake at 180°C for 45 to 50 minutes or until the cake springs back when lightly touched. Leave in tin for 10 minutes before turning on to a cooling rack. When cold dust with sifted icing sugar and second measure of cocoa mixed together.

From top, clockwise:
Honey Cake, Bowls Cake
and Chocolate Cake

18

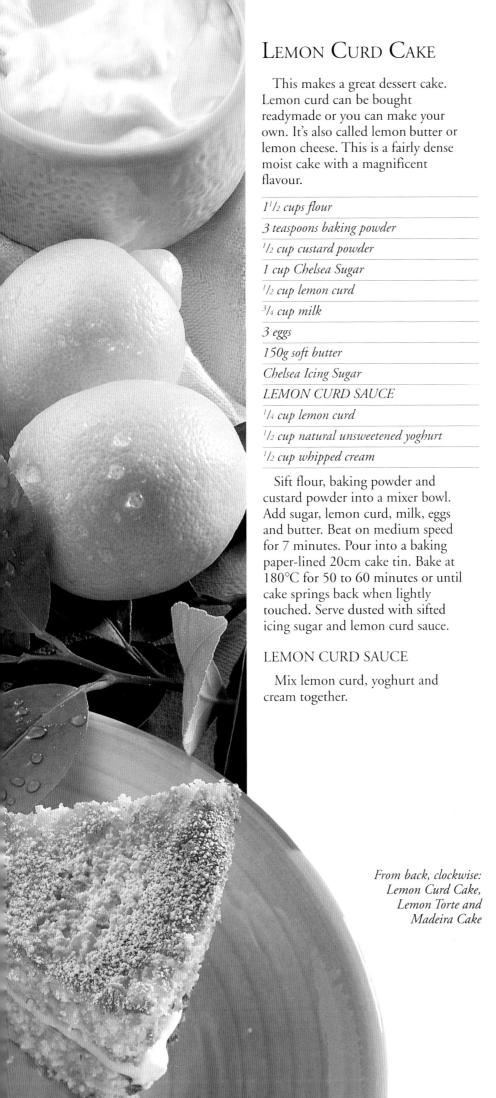

LEMON CURD CAKE

This makes a great dessert cake. Lemon curd can be bought readymade or you can make your own. It's also called lemon butter or lemon cheese. This is a fairly dense moist cake with a magnificent flavour.

1½ cups flour

3 teaspoons baking powder

½ cup custard powder

1 cup Chelsea Sugar

½ cup lemon curd

¾ cup milk

3 eggs

150g soft butter

Chelsea Icing Sugar

LEMON CURD SAUCE

¼ cup lemon curd

½ cup natural unsweetened yoghurt

½ cup whipped cream

Sift flour, baking powder and custard powder into a mixer bowl. Add sugar, lemon curd, milk, eggs and butter. Beat on medium speed for 7 minutes. Pour into a baking paper-lined 20cm cake tin. Bake at 180°C for 50 to 60 minutes or until cake springs back when lightly touched. Serve dusted with sifted icing sugar and lemon curd sauce.

LEMON CURD SAUCE

Mix lemon curd, yoghurt and cream together.

LEMON TORTE

This is one of those special cakes with no flour that can be quickly rustled up for an afternoon tea or dessert. Lemon curd is also called lemon honey or lemon cheese. It can be bought readymade from the jam section in the supermarket. You can double this recipe and fill the cake with lemon cream if wished.

3 eggs

½ cup Chelsea Caster Sugar

1 tablespoon grated lemon rind

3 tablespoons lemon juice

½ cup semolina

Chelsea Icing Sugar

½ cup cream

2 tablespoons lemon curd

Separate the eggs. Beat the egg yolks and sugar with an electric mixer until pale and thick. On a slow speed beat in the lemon rind, juice and semolina until combined. Beat egg whites until stiff and fold into egg yolk mixture using a low mixer speed, or fold in by hand. Pour into a baking paper-lined 20cm round sponge sandwich tin, or two tins if you have doubled the recipe. Bake at 180°C for 30 to 40 minutes or until cake springs back when lightly touched. Leave in tin for 10 minutes before turning onto a cooling rack. Remove paper while still warm. Dust cake with sifted icing sugar. Whip cream until soft and fold in lemon curd. Serve with the cake.

*From back, clockwise:
Lemon Curd Cake,
Lemon Torte and
Madeira Cake*

MADEIRA CAKE

125g soft butter

½ cup Chelsea Sugar

1 teaspoon vanilla essence

2 eggs

1½ cups flour

3 teaspoons baking powder

½ cup milk

Place butter, sugar, vanilla essence, eggs, flour, baking powder and milk in a mixer bowl. Beat on low speed until just combined. Increase speed and beat for 2 minutes. Pour into a baking paper-lined 22cm loaf tin and bake at 180°C for 50 to 60 minutes or until cake springs back when lightly touched. Leave in tin for 10 minutes before turning out onto a cooling rack. Ice if wished.

DATE AND WALNUT CAKE

Dates and walnuts are a scrumptious combination and, topped with this delicious icing, this cake is sure to find favour.

2 cups chopped pitted dates

1 teaspoon baking soda

1¼ cups boiling water

150g butter

½ cup Chelsea Soft Brown Sugar

½ cup chopped walnuts

2 cups flour

1 teaspoon baking powder

1 teaspoon mixed spice

walnut halves to decorate

CARAMEL ICING

2 cups Chelsea Icing Sugar

2 tablespoons hot water

1 tablespoon Chelsea Golden Syrup

1 tablespoon Chelsea Soft Brown Sugar

½ teaspoon vanilla essence

Place dates and baking soda in a bowl. Pour boiling water over. Set aside. Place butter and brown sugar in a saucepan large enough to mix all the ingredients. Heat until butter melts. Remove from heat. Add dates, chopped walnuts, sifted flour, baking powder and mixed spice. Mix with a wooden spoon until combined. Spread into a baking paper-lined 20cm round cake tin. Bake at 180°C for 40 to 45 minutes or until cake springs back when lightly touched. Leave in tin for 10 minutes before turning onto a cooling rack. Ice with caramel icing when cold and decorate with walnut halves.

CARAMEL ICING

Sift icing sugar into a bowl. Mix water and golden syrup together. Add to icing sugar with brown sugar and vanilla essence and mix to form a smooth, spreadable icing.

Date and Walnut Cake, Gingerbread and Apricot Cake

GINGERBREAD

If possible keep the gingerbread for several days before cutting. This develops the flavour.

150g butter

1 cup low fat milk

1 cup Chelsea Golden Syrup

½ cup Chelsea Soft Brown Sugar

2 teaspoons baking soda

2½ cups flour

2½ teaspoons ground ginger

2 teaspoons mixed spice

Place butter, milk, golden syrup and brown sugar in a saucepan large enough to mix all the ingredients. Heat until butter melts. Remove from heat and add baking soda. When frothing stir in sifted flour, ginger and mixed spice. Mix until just smooth. Pour into a baking paper-lined 20cm square cake tin. Bake at 180°C for 45 to 50 minutes or until the gingerbread springs back when lightly touched. Leave in the tin for 10 minutes before turning on to a cooling rack. Serve lightly buttered if wished.

APRICOT CAKE

1½ cups chopped dried apricots

1 cup boiling water

200g butter

¾ cup Chelsea Sugar

3 eggs

¾ teaspoon baking soda

2 cups flour

2 teaspoons baking powder

Place apricots in a bowl. Pour boiling water over. Set aside. Place butter and sugar in a saucepan large enough to mix all the ingredients. Heat until butter melts. Cool, then beat in eggs using a wooden spoon. Drain apricots, reserving ½ cup of the liquid. Dissolve baking soda in the measured apricot liquid. Mix apricot liquid mixture, apricots and sifted flour and baking powder into butter mixture until combined. Pour into a baking paper-lined 20cm round cake tin. Bake at 180°C for 45 to 55 minutes or until cake springs back when lightly touched. Leave to cool in tin for 10 minutes before turning onto a cooling rack. Dust with sifted icing sugar or ice with lemon icing when cold.

CHOCOLATE CHERRY FOREST CAKE

Dust this cake with sifted icing sugar or ice with chocolate icing as an alternative to the jam and flake bars.

150g butter

1 cup chocolate melts

1 cup Chelsea Sugar

$^1/_4$ cup cocoa

3 eggs

1 teaspoon vanilla essence

2 cups flour

2 teaspoons baking powder

1 teaspoon baking soda

1 cup low fat milk

$^3/_4$ cup halved glace cherries

1 tablespoon jam

2 chocolate flake bars

Place butter, chocolate melts, sugar and cocoa in a saucepan large enough to mix all the ingredients. Heat until butter and chocolate melt. Cool slightly. Beat in eggs with a wooden spoon. Add vanilla essence, sifted flour, baking powder, baking soda and milk. Beat until smooth. Pour mixture into a baking paper-lined 20cm round cake tin. Dry cherries on a paper towel and sprinkle over mixture in cake tin. Bake at 180°C for 1$^1/_4$ hours or until cake springs back when lightly touched. Leave in the tin to cool for 10 minutes before turning onto a cooling rack. Brush top of cake with jam while still warm. When cold, decorate with broken flake bars.

WHOLEMEAL CHOCOLATE CAKE

Using wholemeal flour in your baking adds fibre and gives baked goodies a more grainy texture. This is a good everyday chocolate cake. Corn, safflower, grapeseed or any other oil that is not strongly flavoured is suitable for this cake.

1 cup wholemeal flour

1 cup flour

$^1/_4$ cup cocoa

1 teaspoon cinnamon

2 teaspoons baking powder

1 teaspoon baking soda

1 cup Chelsea Soft Brown Sugar

2 eggs

$^3/_4$ cup oil

$^3/_4$ cup water

Mix flours, cocoa, cinnamon, baking powder, baking soda and brown sugar together in a bowl until blended. Make a well in the dry ingredients. Beat eggs, oil and water together in a bowl. Pour into well and mix with a wooden spoon until smooth. Pour into a baking paper-lined 20cm plain or moulded ring tin. Bake at 180°C for 35 to 45 minutes or until cake springs back when lightly touched. Leave in tin for 10 minutes before turning onto a cooling rack.

CHOCOLATE MARBLE CAKE

This cake looks stunning if made in a moulded ring tin.

125g butter

$^3/_4$ cup Chelsea Sugar

3 eggs

$^1/_2$ cup milk

$1^1/_2$ cups flour

3 teaspoons baking powder

2 teaspoons vanilla essence

2 tablespoons cocoa

2 tablespoons boiling water

$^1/_4$ cup dark chocolate melts

$^1/_4$ cup white chocolate melts

Melt butter in a mixer bowl in the microwave or over hot water. Add sugar, eggs, milk, flour, baking powder and vanilla essence to butter. Mix on low speed until combined. Increase speed to medium and beat for 3 minutes or until smooth. Pour half the mixture into a well greased 20cm moulded ring tin. Mix cocoa and water together and mix into remaining half of cake mixture. Pour over plain mixture. Using a fork, squiggle the tines gently through both mixtures to marble. Bake at 160°C for 55 to 60 minutes or until cake springs back when lightly touched. Leave in tin for 10 minutes before turning onto a cooling rack. Melt chocolate melts separately. Drizzle chocolates over cake when cold.

*From left, clockwise:
Chocolate Marble Cake,
Wholemeal Chocolate Cake and
Chocolate Cherry Forest Cake*

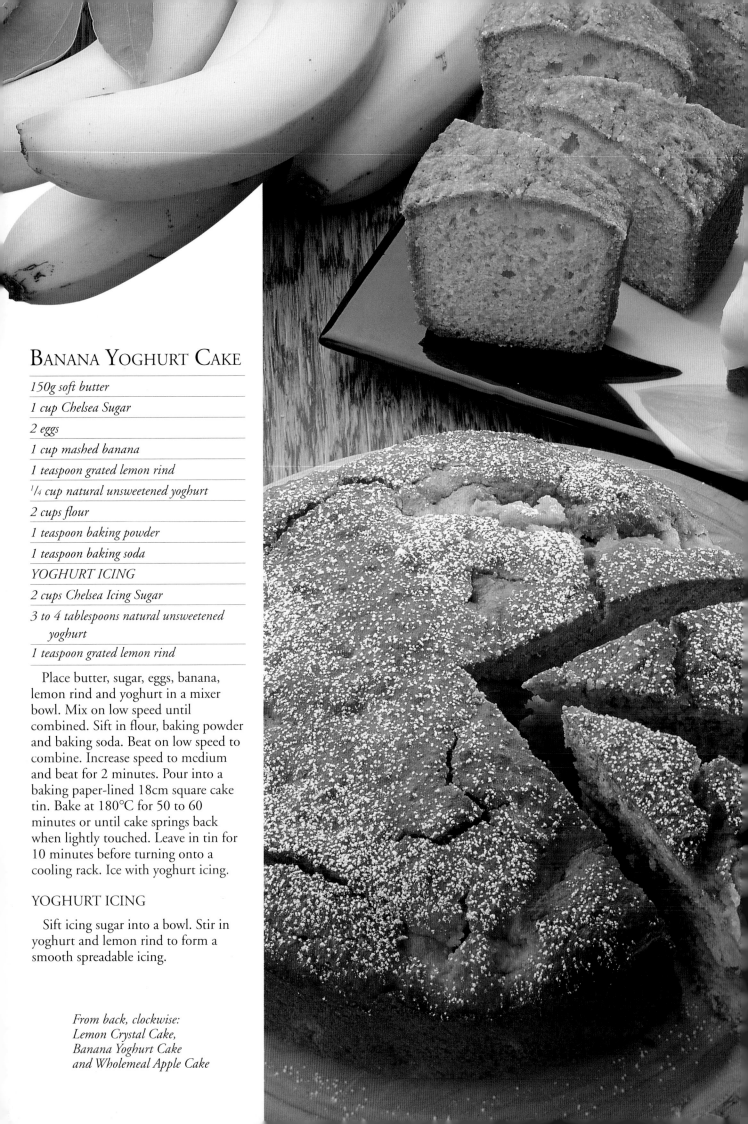

BANANA YOGHURT CAKE

150g soft butter

1 cup Chelsea Sugar

2 eggs

1 cup mashed banana

1 teaspoon grated lemon rind

1/4 cup natural unsweetened yoghurt

2 cups flour

1 teaspoon baking powder

1 teaspoon baking soda

YOGHURT ICING

2 cups Chelsea Icing Sugar

3 to 4 tablespoons natural unsweetened
   yoghurt

1 teaspoon grated lemon rind

Place butter, sugar, eggs, banana,
lemon rind and yoghurt in a mixer
bowl. Mix on low speed until
combined. Sift in flour, baking powder
and baking soda. Beat on low speed to
combine. Increase speed to medium
and beat for 2 minutes. Pour into a
baking paper-lined 18cm square cake
tin. Bake at 180°C for 50 to 60
minutes or until cake springs back
when lightly touched. Leave in tin for
10 minutes before turning onto a
cooling rack. Ice with yoghurt icing.

YOGHURT ICING

Sift icing sugar into a bowl. Stir in
yoghurt and lemon rind to form a
smooth spreadable icing.

From back, clockwise:
Lemon Crystal Cake,
Banana Yoghurt Cake
and Wholemeal Apple Cake

LEMON CRYSTAL CAKE

125g butter

1 cup Chelsea Sugar

3 eggs

2 tablespoons milk

2 teaspoons grated lemon rind

2 cups flour

4 teaspoons baking powder

LEMON SYRUP

¹/₄ cup lemon juice

¹/₄ cup Chelsea Sugar

Place butter and sugar in a saucepan large enough to mix all the ingredients. Heat until butter melts. Beat eggs, milk and lemon rind together until frothy. Mix egg mixture and sifted flour and baking powder into the saucepan. Beat with a wooden spoon until combined. Pour mixture into a well greased or baking paper-lined ring or moulded ring tin. Bake at 180°C for 1 hour or until the cake springs back when lightly touched. Leave in the tin for 10 minutes before turning onto a cooling rack. Pour lemon syrup over and leave until cold.

LEMON SYRUP

Mix lemon juice and sugar together.

WHOLEMEAL APPLE CAKE

Serve this yummy cake warm with soft whipped cream if wished. Use high grade flour or flour suitable for making fruit cakes otherwise the cake will probably sink in the middle. Canned solid pack apples are used in this recipe.

125g butter

¹/₂ cup Chelsea Soft Brown Sugar

2 eggs

³/₄ cup apple juice concentrate

1¹/₂ cups wholemeal flour

1 cup flour

4 teaspoons baking powder

410g can apple slices

Chelsea Icing Sugar

Place butter and brown sugar in a saucepan large enough to mix all the ingredients. Heat, stirring until butter melts. Remove from heat. Beat in eggs and apple juice concentrate until combined. Mix in flours and baking powder using a wooden spoon, mixing until combined. Fold in canned apple. Pour into a baking paper-lined 20cm cake tin. Bake at 180°C for 50 to 60 minutes or until cake springs back when lightly touched. Leave in tin for 10 minutes before turning onto a cooling rack. Dust with sifted icing sugar.

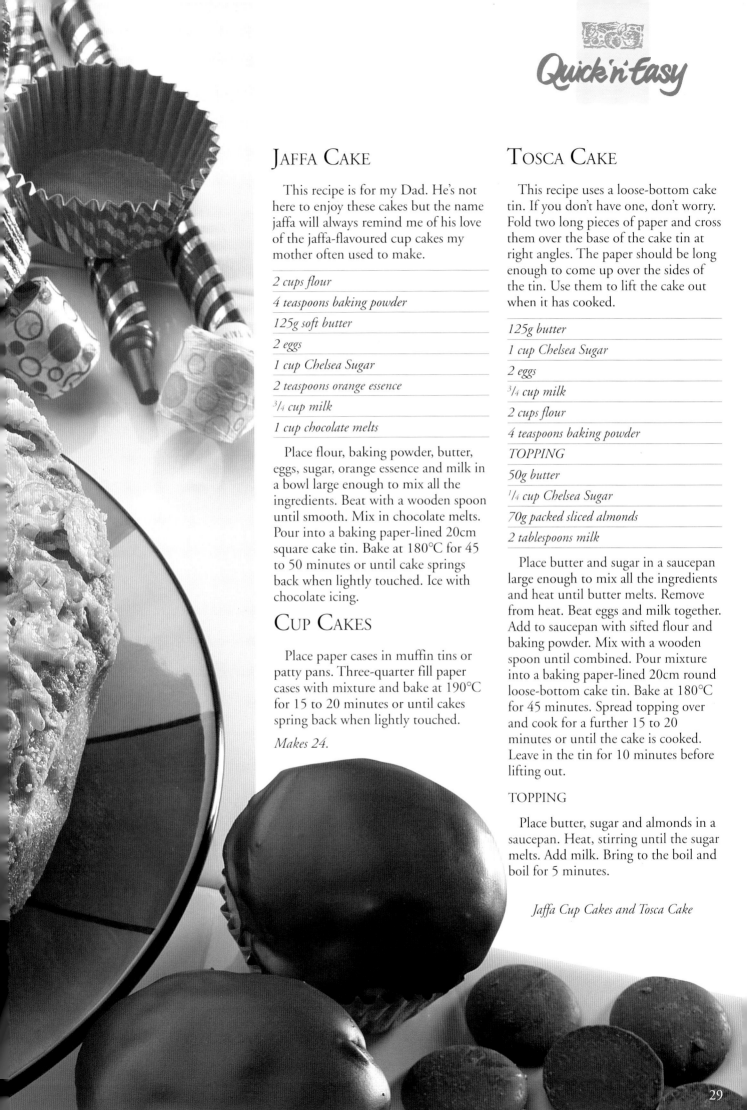

JAFFA CAKE

This recipe is for my Dad. He's not here to enjoy these cakes but the name jaffa will always remind me of his love of the jaffa-flavoured cup cakes my mother often used to make.

2 cups flour

4 teaspoons baking powder

125g soft butter

2 eggs

1 cup Chelsea Sugar

2 teaspoons orange essence

3/4 cup milk

1 cup chocolate melts

Place flour, baking powder, butter, eggs, sugar, orange essence and milk in a bowl large enough to mix all the ingredients. Beat with a wooden spoon until smooth. Mix in chocolate melts. Pour into a baking paper-lined 20cm square cake tin. Bake at 180°C for 45 to 50 minutes or until cake springs back when lightly touched. Ice with chocolate icing.

CUP CAKES

Place paper cases in muffin tins or patty pans. Three-quarter fill paper cases with mixture and bake at 190°C for 15 to 20 minutes or until cakes spring back when lightly touched.

Makes 24.

TOSCA CAKE

This recipe uses a loose-bottom cake tin. If you don't have one, don't worry. Fold two long pieces of paper and cross them over the base of the cake tin at right angles. The paper should be long enough to come up over the sides of the tin. Use them to lift the cake out when it has cooked.

125g butter

1 cup Chelsea Sugar

2 eggs

3/4 cup milk

2 cups flour

4 teaspoons baking powder

TOPPING

50g butter

1/4 cup Chelsea Sugar

70g packed sliced almonds

2 tablespoons milk

Place butter and sugar in a saucepan large enough to mix all the ingredients and heat until butter melts. Remove from heat. Beat eggs and milk together. Add to saucepan with sifted flour and baking powder. Mix with a wooden spoon until combined. Pour mixture into a baking paper-lined 20cm round loose-bottom cake tin. Bake at 180°C for 45 minutes. Spread topping over and cook for a further 15 to 20 minutes or until the cake is cooked. Leave in the tin for 10 minutes before lifting out.

TOPPING

Place butter, sugar and almonds in a saucepan. Heat, stirring until the sugar melts. Add milk. Bring to the boil and boil for 5 minutes.

Jaffa Cup Cakes and Tosca Cake

Quick 'n' Easy

BIG BAKES

There are lots of occasions when one cake or batch of biscuits
just isn't enough.

It may be a school gala, a Plunket cake stall or a "bring and
buy", or perhaps you have to supply baked goodies to an elderly
relative. Then there's always Christmas cakes for gifts.

When you need to supply lots of something baked, don't despair
trying to cope with such a big task. You will be surprised at
what you already have in your kitchen to help you cater for
more than a usual family bake.

The recipes that follow will solve a lot of problems when you are
next asked to contribute to a cake stall or something similar.

Quick'n'Easy

CHRISTMAS CAKE

Use as one large cake or cut into four for small cakes to give as Christmas gifts. Use high grade flour or flour suitable for making fruit cakes.

1kg mixed dried fruit

1 cup flour

400g butter

3 cups Chelsea Soft Brown Sugar

5 eggs

1 tablespoon grated orange rind

1 tablespoon grated lemon rind

2¹/₂ cups flour

3 teaspoons mixed spice

2 teaspoons cinnamon

¹/₂ teaspoon baking soda

¹/₄ cup cold tea

Line the bottom of a 28 x 36cm roasting dish with a layer of baking paper. Layer 4 to 6 layers of brown paper or newspaper for the tin to sit on in the oven. In a large plastic bag mix dried fruit with first measure of flour. Melt butter and brown sugar together in a saucepan large enough to mix all the ingredients. Cool slightly, then beat in eggs with a wooden spoon. Add orange and lemon rinds and sift second measure of flour, mixed spice, cinnamon and baking soda into saucepan and add cold tea. Mix until combined. Spread mixture evenly into the prepared tin. Sit tin on paper in oven and bake at 150°C for 1¹/₂ hours, or until an inserted skewer comes out clean. Leave cake to cool in tin. Trim edges and cut into four cakes.

Christmas Cake

CATHEDRAL WINDOW CAKES

These cakes make a great Christmas gift. They are not cheap to make but could solve a gift problem. Measure loaf tins from the top edges and use high grade flour or flour suitable for fruit cakes.

1kg mixed glace fruits such as pears, pineapple, cherries, apricots

350g blanched almonds

650g brazil nuts

9 eggs

1¹/₂ cups Chelsea Caster Sugar

3 teaspoons vanilla essence

¹/₂ cup brandy

2¹/₄ cups flour

2 teaspoons baking powder

2 teaspoons mixed spice

Chop the glace fruits if large. Mix fruit, almonds and brazil nuts together. In a large bowl beat eggs, caster sugar, vanilla essence and brandy together. Fold sifted flour, baking powder and mixed spice into egg mixture. Mix fruit and nuts into egg mixture until combined. Divide mixture evenly between four baking paper-lined 20 x 10cm loaf tins. Bake at 160°C for 1¹/₂ hours or until an inserted skewer comes out clean. Cool in tins. Remove lining paper and wrap in foil or seal in a plastic bag until ready to wrap for giving.

Makes 4 loaf-shaped cakes.

Fruit Fingers,
"Oh Crumbs" Biscuits
and Cathedral
Window Cakes

FRUIT FINGERS

4¹/₂ cups mixed fruit such as dates, raisins, sultanas

³/₄ cup Chelsea Soft Brown Sugar

50g butter

2 teaspoons mixed spice

1 cup orange juice

2 cups soft breadcrumbs

2 x 350g rolls pre-rolled flaky pastry

2 tablespoons Chelsea Caster Sugar

Place the mixed fruit, brown sugar, butter, mixed spice and orange juice in a saucepan. Bring to the boil, stirring until butter melts. Cover and remove from heat. Set aside to cool. Mix breadcrumbs into fruit mixture. Unroll one packet of pastry onto a lightly floured oven tray. Spread fruit mixture over pastry to within 1cm of the edge. Dampen edges with water. Unroll second packet of pastry over the top of the fruit filling. Press edges together. Prick top pastry with a fork. Sprinkle sugar over. Bake at 210°C for 15 to 20 minutes or until pastry is golden. When cold, cut into fingers.

"OH CRUMBS" BISCUITS

Top these biscuits with a walnut if you feel generous.

200g soft butter

1¹/₂ cups Chelsea Sugar

2 tablespoons Chelsea Golden Syrup

2 teaspoons vanilla essence

2 eggs

1¹/₄ cups flour

2 cups coconut

1¹/₂ cups toasted breadcrumbs

2 teaspoons baking powder

Place butter, sugar, golden syrup, vanilla essence and eggs in a mixer bowl. Mix to combine. Add flour, coconut, breadcrumbs and baking powder to the bowl and mix on low speed until combined. Roll tablespoonsful into balls. Place on a greased oven tray. Flatten with a fork. Bake at 180°C for 10 to 15 minutes or until golden.

Makes about 70.

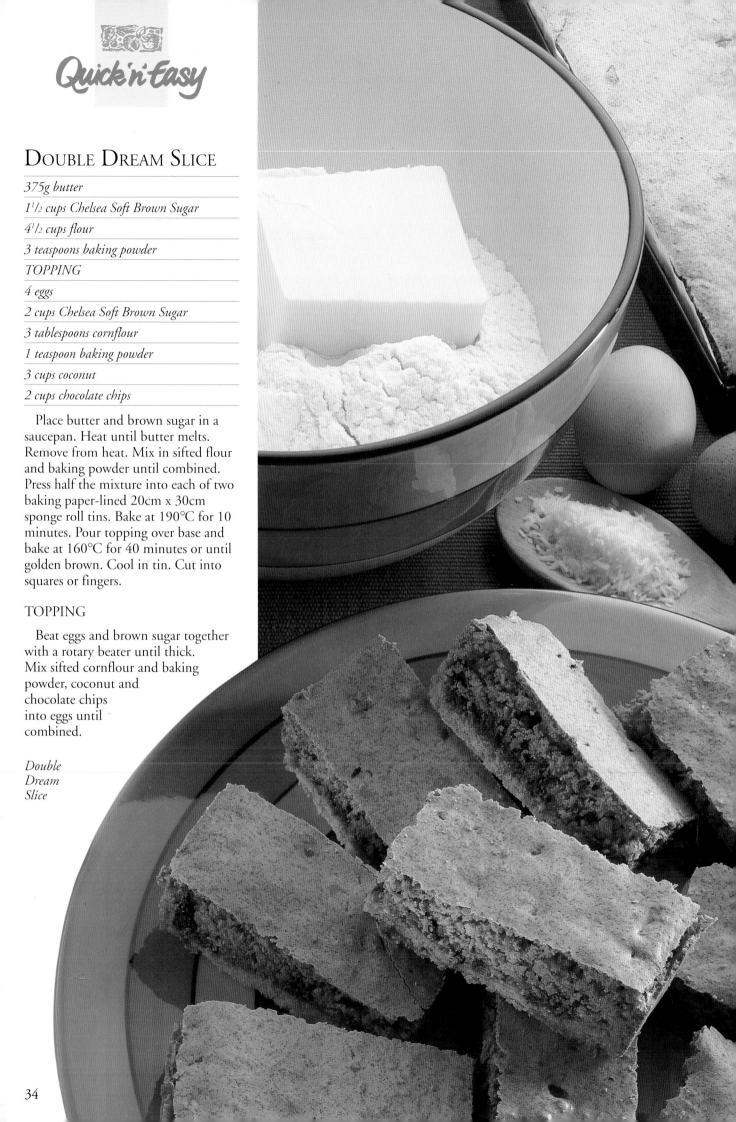

DOUBLE DREAM SLICE

375g butter

1½ cups Chelsea Soft Brown Sugar

4½ cups flour

3 teaspoons baking powder

TOPPING

4 eggs

2 cups Chelsea Soft Brown Sugar

3 tablespoons cornflour

1 teaspoon baking powder

3 cups coconut

2 cups chocolate chips

Place butter and brown sugar in a saucepan. Heat until butter melts. Remove from heat. Mix in sifted flour and baking powder until combined. Press half the mixture into each of two baking paper-lined 20cm x 30cm sponge roll tins. Bake at 190°C for 10 minutes. Pour topping over base and bake at 160°C for 40 minutes or until golden brown. Cool in tin. Cut into squares or fingers.

TOPPING

Beat eggs and brown sugar together with a rotary beater until thick. Mix sifted cornflour and baking powder, coconut and chocolate chips into eggs until combined.

*Double
Dream
Slice*

RAISIN AND LEMON CAKE

1kg raisins
$^1/_2$ cup lemon juice
400g butter
4 eggs
2 cups Chelsea Sugar
2 teaspoons grated lemon rind
$4^1/_2$ cups flour
5 teaspoons baking powder
1 cup milk

Place raisins, lemon juice and butter in a saucepan large enough to mix all the ingredients. Heat until butter melts. Cool slightly. Beat in eggs with a wooden spoon. Add sugar, lemon rind, sifted flour and baking powder and milk to saucepan. Mix until well combined. Pour into a baking paper-lined 28 x 36cm roasting dish. Bake at 160°C for 1 hour or until cake springs back when lightly touched. Ice with lemon icing if wished. Cut into four cakes.

Raisin and Lemon Cake

LINZER CAKE

Have the baking paper over the edges of the tin to help lift the cake out.

250g butter

3¹/₂ cups Chelsea Soft Brown Sugar

4 eggs

2 teaspoons baking soda

2 cups milk

4³/₄ cups flour

4 teaspoons cinnamon

2 teaspoons mixed spice

6 teaspoons baking powder

1 cup raspberry jam

1 cup finely chopped walnuts

Chelsea Icing Sugar

Place butter and brown sugar in a saucepan large enough to mix all the ingredients. Heat until butter melts. Cool slightly. Beat in eggs with a wooden spoon. Dissolve baking soda in milk. Sift flour, cinnamon, mixed spice and baking powder into saucepan. Add milk mixture and mix with a wooden spoon until the batter is smooth. Place half the mixture in a baking paper-lined 27 x 34cm roasting dish. Warm raspberry jam in the microwave or over hot water and spread over batter in tin. Sprinkle walnuts over. Top with remaining mixture. Bake at 180°C for 1 hour or until cake springs back when lightly touched. Leave in tin for 10 minutes before turning onto a large cooling rack. When cold, dust with sifted icing sugar and cut into four cakes or into squares.

CORNFLAKE CRUNCHIES

200g butter

1 cup Chelsea Soft Brown Sugar

1 cup Chelsea Sugar

3 eggs

2 cups coconut

5 cups lightly crushed cornflakes

Place butter and sugars in a saucepan. Heat until butter melts. Cool slightly then beat in eggs using a wooden spoon. Stir in coconut and cornflakes until combined. Drop tablespoonsful on to greased oven trays. Bake at 180°C for 10 to 15 minutes or until golden. When starting to firm, transfer to a cooling rack. Store in an airtight container.

Makes about 66.

CHOCOLATE CAKE

4 eggs

2 cups milk

2 teaspoons vanilla essence

250g soft butter

2 cups strong black coffee

1¹/₂ cups Chelsea Sugar

4 cups flour

2 teaspoons baking powder

4 teaspoons baking soda

1 cup cocoa

CHOCOLATE ICING

3 cups Chelsea Icing Sugar

6 tablespoons cocoa

50g soft butter

About 6 tablespoons hot water

Place eggs, milk, vanilla essence, butter, coffee and sugar in a mixer bowl. Mix until combined. Add sifted flour, baking powder, baking soda and cocoa. Mix on low speed until combined, then increase speed to medium and beat for 2 minutes or until a smooth batter forms. Pour batter into a baking paper-lined 28 x 36cm roasting dish. Bake at 180°C for 1 hour or until cake springs back when lightly touched. Leave in tin for 10 minutes before turning out onto a large cooling rack. Ice with chocolate icing when cold. Cut into four individual cakes or into squares.

CHOCOLATE ICING

Sift icing sugar and cocoa into a bowl. Add butter and water and mix until smooth.

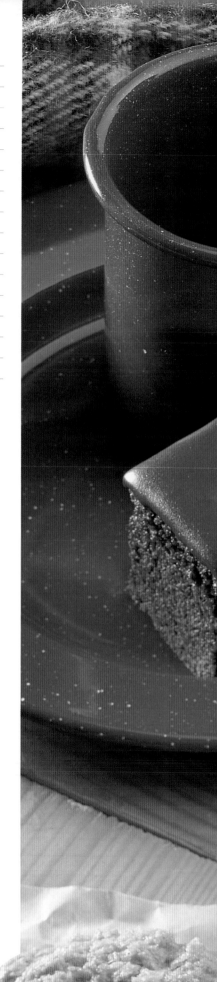

Chocolate Cake, Linzer Cake and Cornflake Crunchies

Quick'n'Easy

Quick 'n' Easy

BISCUITS

A batch of biscuits was once no trouble to rustle up but with the

pressures on our time in the 1990s we have to consider faster

ways to provide something to fill the biscuit tins.

Yes, you can always buy a packet of biscuits but there is

something very satisfying about baking your own and you just

can't beat that lovely smell of home baking.

Biscuits made without the drudgery of creaming the butter and

sugar are not as short in their texture as those made by

traditional methods. They taste just as good though and the

time you save is worth a slightly less short biscuit.

Using a standard measuring spoon helps give good-shaped,

even-sized biscuits.

Yo Yos

Make these biscuits go further by not sticking them together. Place half a teaspoon of raspberry jam in the centre of each biscuit halfway through cooking.

200g butter

$^1/_2$ cup Chelsea Icing Sugar

1 teaspoon vanilla essence

$1^3/_4$ cups flour

$^1/_4$ cup custard powder

$^1/_2$ cup raspberry jam

Melt the butter in a saucepan large enough to mix all the ingredients. Beat in the icing sugar and vanilla essence. Sift the flour and custard powder into the saucepan. Mix until combined. Using a measuring spoon, measure tablespoonsful of mixture onto a greased oven tray. Flatten with a fork. Bake at 180°C for 15 to 20 minutes or until just starting to colour. Cool on a cooling rack. When cold, spread half the biscuits with raspberry jam. Stick an unjammed biscuit on top.

Makes 13 pairs.

Rock Cakes

1 cup flour

$^1/_2$ cup wholemeal flour

1 teaspoon baking powder

100g butter

$^1/_4$ cup Chelsea Soft Brown Sugar

$^1/_2$ cup raisins

1 egg

$^1/_4$ cup milk

1 teaspoon grated lemon rind

1 tablespoon Chelsea Raw Sugar

Mix flours and baking powder together in a bowl large enough to mix all the ingredients. Cut in the butter until mixture resembles coarse crumbs. Mix in brown sugar and raisins. Beat egg, milk and lemon rind until combined. Mix into dry ingredients, adding extra milk if necessary, to make a stiff dough. Place rough rounds on a greased oven tray. Sprinkle with raw sugar. Bake at 200°C for 10 to 15 minutes or until lightly golden. Cool on a cooling rack.

Makes 12.

Rock Cakes and Yo Yos

Quick 'n' Easy

ABSOLUTELY AMAZING PEANUT BUTTER BIKKIES

This is no misprint. There are only three ingredients in these biscuits.

1 egg

1 cup crunchy peanut butter

1 cup Chelsea Sugar

Beat egg. Mix egg, peanut butter and sugar together. Roll two tablespoonsful of mixture into balls. Place on a greased baking tray and flatten with a fork, allowing room for spreading. Bake at 180°C for 10 minutes or until golden.

Makes about 12.

PEIGI'S CORNFLAKE BISCUITS

These biscuits are very moreish, especially with a cup of afternoon tea.

150g butter

$^1/_2$ cup Chelsea Sugar

1 egg

$^1/_4$ cup sultanas

$1^1/_2$ cups flour

1 teaspoon baking powder

About 2 cups cornflakes

Melt butter and sugar in a saucepan large enough to mix all the ingredients. Cool slightly then mix in the egg, sultanas, sifted flour and baking powder until combined. Lightly crush cornflakes. Using a measuring spoon, measure heaped tablespoonsful of mixture. Drop into cornflakes and toss to coat. Place on a greased oven tray and flatten with a fork, allowing room for spreading. Bake at 180°C for 15 minutes or until golden.

Makes about 20.

Peigi's Cornflake Biscuits and Absolutely Amazing Peanut Butter Bikkies

Italian Biscotti

Add $^1/_2$ cup shelled pistachio nuts to this recipe if you wish.

1 x 70g packet blanched almonds

$^1/_2$ cup shelled pistachio nuts

2 cups flour

1 teaspoon baking powder

Pinch salt

$^1/_2$ cup Chelsea Caster Sugar

1 teaspoon vanilla essence

2 eggs

1 egg white

Toast almonds at 180°C for 5 to 10 minutes or until pale golden yellow. Allow to cool then chop roughly. Sift flour, baking powder and salt into a mixing bowl. Add caster sugar and stir until combined. Lightly beat vanilla essence and eggs together then add to dry ingredients. Mix until well combined. Turn onto a lightly floured surface and work in the nuts. Add more flour if necessary until a firm dough is reached. Divide mixture in half and shape into logs about 5cm wide. Place on a greased oven tray. Lightly beat egg white then brush each log with egg white. Bake at 180°C for 35 minutes or until cooked through. Allow to cool slightly then cut each log on the diagonal into 1cm wide slices. Place slices on an oven tray. Reduce temperature to 150°C and bake for a further 10 minutes or until dry.

Makes about 40.

Savoury Corn Chip Cheese Biscuits

These biscuits are a simple goodie to make to serve with drinks. They bubble at the sides on cooking but don't panic, they are fine. They are best served fresh.

100g jalapeno corn chips

50g butter

1 egg

1 $^1/_2$ cups grated tasty cheese

$^1/_4$ cup flour

Crush chips until they are about the size of soft breadcrumbs. Melt the butter in a saucepan large enough to mix all the ingredients. Mix in crushed chips, egg, cheese and flour. Mix well. Using a measuring spoon, measure tablespoonsful onto a greased baking tray. Flatten with the palm of your hand. Bake at 180°C for 10 to 15 minutes or until lightly golden.

Makes 24.

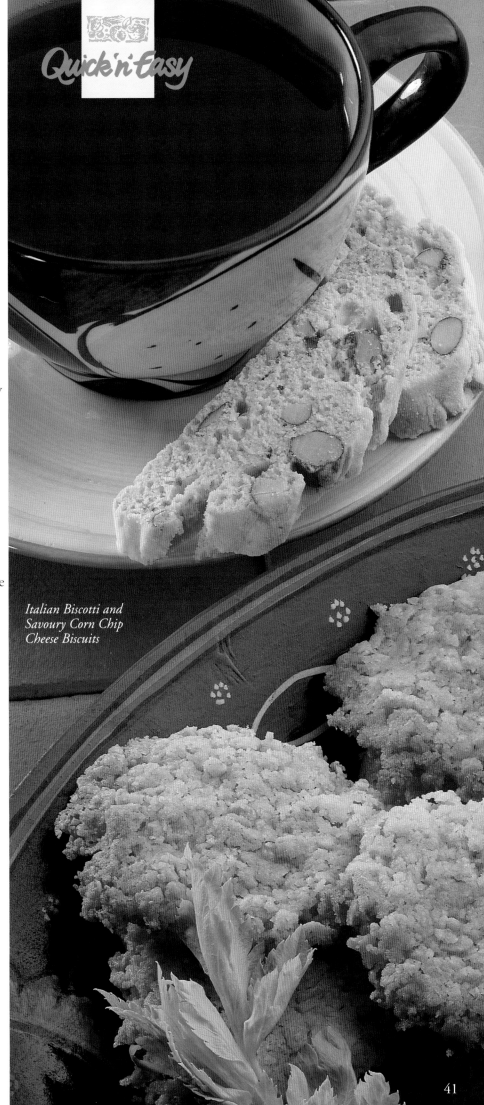

Italian Biscotti and Savoury Corn Chip Cheese Biscuits

41

Quick'n'Easy

CRUNCHOATLOTS

150g butter

2 tablespoons Chelsea Golden Syrup

³/₄ cup Chelsea Soft Brown Sugar

¹/₂ cup coconut

2 cups rolled oats

¹/₂ cup flour

Melt butter, golden syrup and brown sugar in a saucepan large enough to mix all the ingredients. Mix in coconut, oats and flour until combined. Using a measuring spoon, roll tablespoonsful into balls. Place on a greased oven tray allowing room for spreading. Flatten with a spoon. Bake at 180°C for 10 minutes or until lightly browned. Cool on a cooling rack.

Makes 26.

ALMOND MELTS

150g butter

³/₄ cup Chelsea Sugar

1 teaspoon almond essence

1 ¹/₄ cups flour

1 teaspoon baking powder

¹/₄ cup slivered almonds

Melt butter in a saucepan large enough to mix all the ingredients. Mix in sugar and almond essence. Sift flour and baking powder into saucepan. Using a measuring spoon, measure tablespoonsful of mixture and roll into balls. Place on a greased oven tray. Flatten with the palm of your hand. Press a few almonds onto the surface. Bake at 190°C for 15 minutes or until lightly golden.

Makes about 24.

Crunchoatlots,
Chocolate Biscuits,
Almond Melts and
Speedy Shrewsbury Biscuits

CHOCOLATE BISCUITS

200g butter
1 cup Chelsea Sugar
1/4 cup cocoa
1 egg
2 cups flour
2 teaspoons baking powder
1/4 cup chocolate melts

Melt butter with sugar and cocoa in a saucepan large enough to mix all the ingredients. Cool slightly then beat in egg with a wooden spoon until combined. Sift flour and baking powder into the saucepan. Mix until combined. Using a measuring spoon, measure tablespoonsful of mixture and roll into balls. Place on a greased oven tray. Flatten with a fork in a criss-cross pattern. Bake at 180°C for 10 to 15 minutes or until lightly browned. Cool on a cooling rack. Melt chocolate in the microwave or over hot water. Drizzle off the tines of a fork over the biscuits. Leave until chocolate sets.

Makes about 36.

SPEEDY SHREWSBURY BISCUITS

When travelling I always find myself in the kitchenware shops. I found the cutter used for these biscuits in Munich. There are many things in the kitchen that can be used to cut the same effect.

400g packet sweet short pastry
Raspberry jam
Chelsea Icing Sugar

Roll the pastry out on a lightly floured board. Using a 6cm biscuit cutter, cut pastry into rounds. Using an *hors-d'oeuvre* cutter, the end of a piping nozzle or something else with a small hole that can be used for cutting, cut one or more holes in half the biscuits. Place rounds on a floured oven tray. Bake at 190°C for 10 minutes or until lightly golden. Cool on a cooling rack. Spread the biscuits without the hole with jam almost to the edges. Top with holed biscuits. Dust with sifted icing sugar.

Makes 16.

43

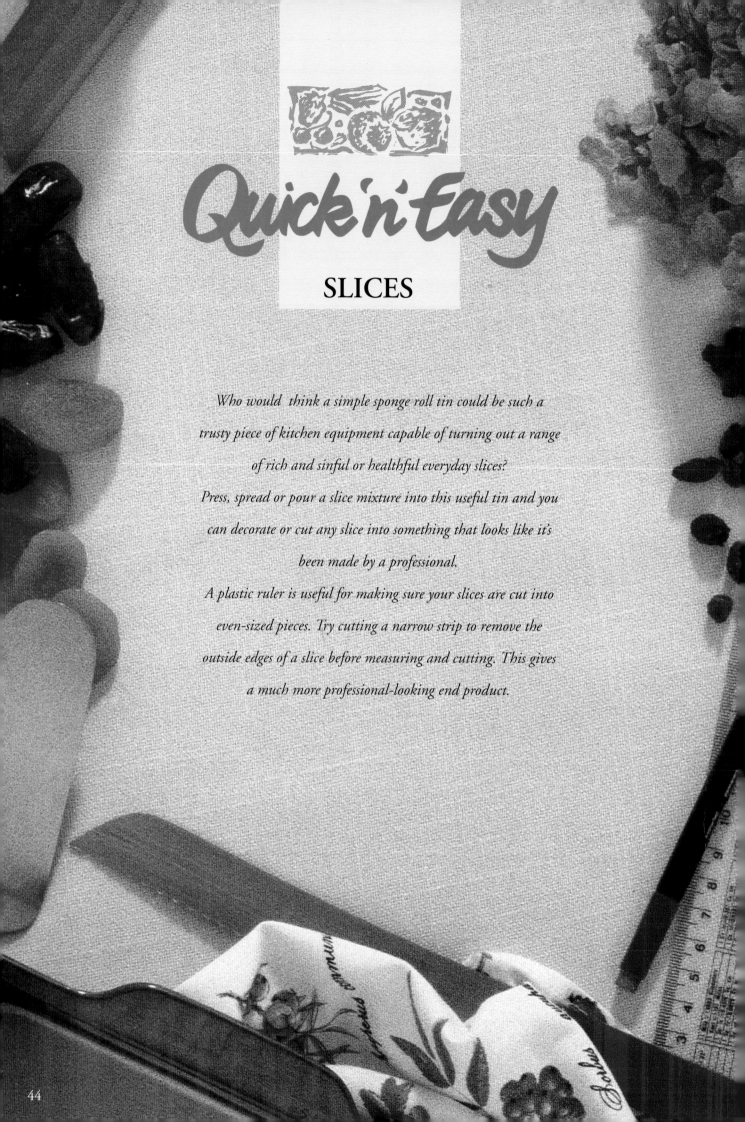

Quick 'n' Easy

SLICES

Who would think a simple sponge roll tin could be such a

trusty piece of kitchen equipment capable of turning out a range

of rich and sinful or healthful everyday slices?

Press, spread or pour a slice mixture into this useful tin and you

can decorate or cut any slice into something that looks like it's

been made by a professional.

A plastic ruler is useful for making sure your slices are cut into

even-sized pieces. Try cutting a narrow strip to remove the

outside edges of a slice before measuring and cutting. This gives

a much more professional-looking end product.

Quick 'n' Easy

COFFEE BROWNIE

200g butter

1¼ cups Chelsea Soft Brown Sugar

2 teaspoons vanilla essence

4 eggs

2 tablespoons instant coffee

2 tablespoons hot water

1¼ cups flour

1 teaspoon baking powder

Chelsea Icing Sugar

Melt butter in a saucepan large enough to mix all the ingredients. Stir in brown sugar, vanilla essence and eggs. Beat with a wooden spoon until combined. Dissolve the coffee in the hot water. Mix into the butter mixture. Sift the flour and baking powder into the saucepan and mix to combine. Pour into a greased 20 x 30cm sponge roll tin. Bake at 180°C for 25 to 30 minutes or until brownie springs back when lightly touched. Cut into squares while still warm. Dust with sifted icing sugar.

MUM'S PINK FINGER

This isn't quite like my Mum used to make it but it tastes just about as good in half the preparation time.

400g packet sweet short pastry

1 cup raspberry jam

RASPBERRY ICING

1½ cups Chelsea Icing Sugar

1 teaspoon raspberry essence

2 to 3 tablespoons hot water

Cut pastry in half. Roll one half out on a lightly floured board to 3mm thickness. Spread with raspberry jam to within 1cm of pastry edge. Roll out second pastry half and, using the rolling pin to lift the pastry, place on top of the jammed half. Press the edges together. Bake at 190°C for 15 minutes or until lightly golden. Remove from oven. Cool, then ice with raspberry icing. Cut into fingers.

RASPBERRY ICING

Sift icing sugar into a bowl. Add raspberry essence and enough hot water to form a smooth, spreadable icing.

Coffee Brownie and Mum's Pink Finger

SWISS JAM SLICE

150g soft butter

¹/₂ cup Chelsea Icing Sugar

1¹/₂ cups flour

¹/₂ cup cornflour

¹/₄ cup apricot jam

Place butter, icing sugar, flour and cornflour in a large bowl. Mix with a wooden spoon or in a mixer until combined. Press mixture into a greased 20 x 30cm sponge roll tin. Make a groove in the mixture with a knife 2cm in from one long side of the tin. Make four more grooves 4cm apart from the first groove. Bake at 160°C for 8 to 10 minutes. Spoon a strip of warmed apricot jam down each groove. Cut into fingers between the grooves while warm.

QUICK CUSTARD SLICE

Custard Slice has to be an all-time favourite. When this quick way of making a custard slice jumped into my head, I had no idea if it would work. It does and is so quick to make. Use a loose-bottom tin for this recipe if you have one. The custard must be at room temperature or warmed, otherwise the gelatin will form lumps if it goes into cold custard.

2 sheets pre-rolled flaky pastry

4 teaspoons gelatin

2 tablespoons water

1 litre carton prepared custard

CHOCOLATE ICING

1¹/₂ cups Chelsea Icing Sugar

2 tablespoons cocoa

2 tablespoons melted butter

4 tablespoons hot water

Place pastry sheets on an oven tray. Prick very thoroughly with a fork and bake at 200°C for 10 to 15 minutes or until golden. Cool, then trim to fit a 20cm square shallow tin. Mix the gelatin and water together. Leave to swell for 2 to 3 minutes. Heat in the microwave for 20 to 30 seconds to dissolve or dissolve over hot water. Mix into the custard. Make four 40cm long folded paper lifters by taking four pieces of greaseproof or wax paper and folding them lengthwise into four. Use two lifters across each side, pushing into the base and corners of the tin. Place one trimmed pastry sheet into the lifter-lined tin. Pour custard onto the pastry. Top with second trimmed sheet. Refrigerate until custard sets. Ice with chocolate icing and cut into squares or fingers.

CHOCOLATE ICING

Sift icing sugar and cocoa into a bowl. Mix in butter and enough hot water to make a smooth spreadable icing.

Swiss Jam Slice and Quick Custard Slice

47

CHOCOLATE ORANGE AND DATE SLICE

This is a wet mixture, so don't be alarmed.

125g butter

³/₄ cup Chelsea Soft Brown Sugar

¹/₄ cup cocoa

3 eggs

2 teaspoons grated orange rind

1¹/₂ cups flour

2 teaspoons baking powder

³/₄ cup orange juice

1 cup chopped dates

Melt butter in a saucepan large enough to mix all the ingredients. Mix in brown sugar, cocoa, eggs and orange rind. Beat until combined. Sift flour and baking powder into saucepan. Add orange juice and dates and mix until combined. Spread mixture into a greased 20 x 30cm sponge roll tin. Bake at 180°C for 30 to 35 minutes or until cooked. Ice with chocolate icing or dust with sifted icing sugar. Cut into squares or fingers.

SPICY BRAN SLICE

Add chopped nuts or dried fruit to this slice if wished.

150g butter

¹/₂ cup Chelsea Soft Brown Sugar

1 egg

1¹/₂ cups baking bran

¹/₂ cup flour

³/₄ cup wholemeal flour

1 teaspoon mixed spice

1 teaspoon cinnamon

1 teaspoon baking powder

Melt butter in a saucepan large enough to mix all the ingredients. Mix in brown sugar and egg until combined. Add bran to saucepan. Sift flour, mixed spice, cinnamon and baking powder into saucepan. Add wholemeal flour and mix until combined. Spread into a greased 20 x 30cm sponge roll tin. Bake at 180°C for 15 to 20 minutes or until slice is golden and cooked. Cut into bars while still warm.

*Spicy Bran Slice (back left),
Savoury Cheese Straw Slice,
Oatmeal Slice and Chocolate
Orange and Date Slice*

SAVOURY CHEESE STRAW SLICE

Making goodies to serve with drinks is always such a time-consuming fiddle. Here's a slice that provides a quick and delicious savoury to serve as finger food.

1³/4 cups flour
1/4 teaspoon salt
1/4 teaspoon cayenne pepper
100g butter
1¹/2 cups grated tasty cheese
2 eggs
1/2 cup grated tasty cheese
2 tablespoons grated parmesan cheese
2 tablespoons sesame seeds

Sift flour, salt and cayenne pepper into a bowl. Rub in butter until mixture resembles coarse breadcrumbs. Mix in first measure of cheese. Lightly beat eggs and mix in enough egg to form a stiff dough. Knead. Press dough into a greased 20 x 30cm sponge roll tin. Sprinkle over second measure of cheese, parmesan cheese and sesame seeds. Bake at 190°C for 15 to 20 minutes or until golden and cooked. Using a clean ruler to measure, cut slice into 1cm wide strips lengthwise and in half crosswise while still warm.

OATMEAL SLICE

This is a plain slice that goes well with jam, cheese and fruit.

100g butter
1/2 cup Chelsea Raw Sugar
1¹/2 cups wholemeal flour
2 teaspoons baking powder
1/4 teaspoon salt
1/2 cup oatmeal
3 tablespoons milk
2 tablespoons oatmeal

Melt butter and raw sugar in a saucepan large enough to mix all the ingredients. Mix in flour, baking powder, salt, first measure of oatmeal and milk until combined. Press into a greased 20 x 30cm sponge roll tin. Dust with second measure of oatmeal, pressing lightly onto surface of slice. Bake at 190°C for 20 to 25 minutes or until lightly golden and cooked. Cut into fingers while still warm. Serve with butter, jam and cheese.

49

LOUISE CAKE

Here's my quick mix version of an old favourite.

100g butter

¼ cup Chelsea Sugar

2 eggs

1½ cups flour

2 teaspoons baking powder

½ cup raspberry jam

½ cup Chelsea Sugar

½ cup coconut

Melt butter in a saucepan large enough to mix all the ingredients. Stir in first measure of sugar. Separate eggs. Add yolks to saucepan and mix until combined. Sift the flour and baking powder into the saucepan. Mix to combine. Spread mixture into a greased 20 x 30cm sponge roll tin. Spread jam over base. Beat egg whites until stiff. Mix in second measure of sugar and coconut. Spread over jam. Bake at 180°C for 25 to 30 minutes or until cooked and golden. Cut into squares or fingers while still warm.

FLORENTINE SLICE

150g butter

¾ cup Chelsea Sugar

70g packet sliced almonds

½ cup raisins

½ cup glace cherries

1 cup flour

1 teaspoon baking powder

¼ cup chocolate melts

Melt butter and sugar in a saucepan large enough to mix all the ingredients. Remove from heat and add almonds, raisins and cherries. Sift flour and baking powder into the saucepan and mix until combined. Spread into a greased 20cm square shallow tin. Bake at 180°C for 25 minutes or until golden and cooked. Melt chocolate in microwave or over hot water. Drizzle over slice while still warm. Cut into squares or fingers while warm.

CARAMEL NUT BROWNIE

250g butter

$^1/_4$ cup Chelsea Golden Syrup

1 cup Chelsea Soft Brown Sugar

4 eggs

$1^1/_4$ cups flour

1 teaspoon baking powder

1 teaspoon vanilla essence

$^1/_2$ cup chopped walnuts

CARAMEL ICING

$1^1/_2$ cups Chelsea Icing Sugar

2 tablespoons butter

1 tablespoon Chelsea Golden Syrup

$^1/_4$ teaspoon vanilla essence

Melt the butter, golden syrup and brown sugar in a saucepan large enough to mix all the ingredients. Remove from heat and cool slightly. Add the eggs and beat with a wooden spoon until the mixture is smooth. Sift the flour and baking powder into the saucepan. Add the vanilla essence and walnuts. Mix to combine. Pour into a greased 20 x 30cm sponge roll tin. Bake at 180°C for 25 to 30 minutes or until brownie springs back when lightly touched. Ice with caramel icing while still warm then cut into squares or bars.

CARAMEL ICING

Sift icing sugar into a bowl. Melt butter. Add butter, golden syrup and vanilla essence to icing sugar. Mix to form a smooth icing, adding a little hot water if necessary.

Florentine Slice (left),
Caramel Nut Brownie
and Louise Cake

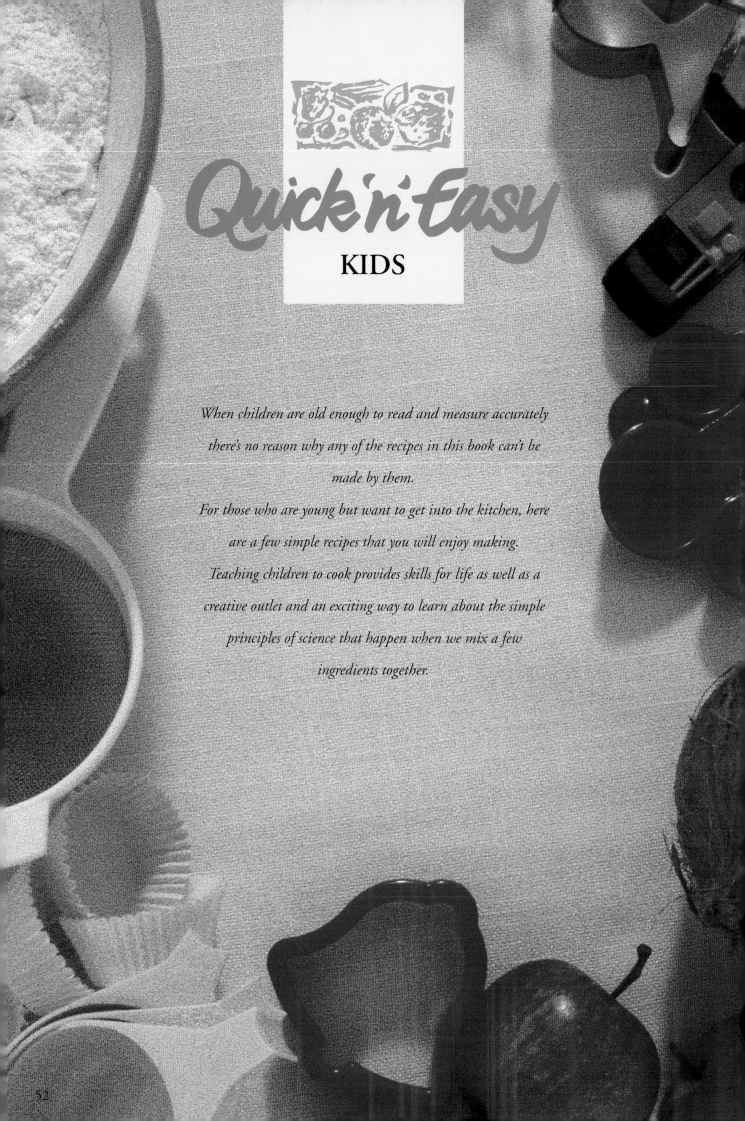

Quick 'n' Easy

KIDS

When children are old enough to read and measure accurately there's no reason why any of the recipes in this book can't be made by them.

For those who are young but want to get into the kitchen, here are a few simple recipes that you will enjoy making.

Teaching children to cook provides skills for life as well as a creative outlet and an exciting way to learn about the simple principles of science that happen when we mix a few ingredients together.

Quick 'n' Easy

COCONUT ICEBERGS

1 egg white

¼ cup Chelsea Sugar

1 cup coconut

Using a fork, lightly beat the egg white. The egg white is beaten enough when there are no stringy bits of egg white hanging off the fork. Mix in the sugar and coconut. Wet the inside of an egg cup. Firmly pack some of the egg mixture into the egg cup. Turn onto a greased oven tray. Bake at 180°C for 6 to 8 minutes.

Makes 8.

TIM'S LAMINGTON CAKE

Let Mum or Dad guide you on how much water to add to the icing for this recipe. The icing needs to be about the thickness of runny cream.

200g piece of sponge

3 tablespoons cocoa

2½ cups Chelsea Icing Sugar

¼ to ½ cup hot water

¼ teaspoon vanilla essence

About 1 cup coconut

Place the sponge in the freezer for 15 minutes before you are ready to make the lamington cake. Sift cocoa and icing sugar into a bowl. Add water and vanilla essence and mix to form a smooth thin icing. Pour the icing into a sponge roll tin. Cut sponge into two 7cm wide strips. Alternatively, to make individual lamingtons, cut into 6 even-sized squares. Place the sponge into the icing. Carefully turn over, using clean hands, until the sponge is coated with icing. Spoon icing over the ends of the sponge. Sprinkle coconut into another sponge roll tin or onto a piece of paper. Carefully lift the icing-coated sponge over to coat with coconut, pressing coconut onto the icing. Lift onto a cooling rack and leave to set. To serve, cut into slices.

Makes two 18cm long lamington cakes, or 6 lamingtons.

Coconut Icebergs and Tim's Lamington Cake

Quick 'n' Easy

FRUIT AND NUT CHOCOLATE UNCOOKED CAKE

If you don't like raisins or nuts, leave them out of this recipe or replace them with something you do like.

250g packet malt biscuits
100g butter
¼ cup Chelsea Sugar
3 tablespoons cocoa
1 egg
1 teaspoon vanilla essence
½ cup raisins
½ cup chopped walnuts

Roughly chop the biscuits until they are coarse crumbs in a food processor or put the biscuits in a strong plastic bag and crush with a rolling pin. Make sure you secure the end of the bag to stop the crumbs coming out. Heat the butter, sugar and cocoa in a saucepan large enough to mix all the ingredients, until the butter melts. Remove from the heat. Cool. Using a wooden spoon, beat in the egg and vanilla essence until there are no stringy bits of egg white hanging off the end of the spoon. Add the crumbs, raisins and walnuts. Mix until well combined. Spread the mixture evenly in a 16cm square cake tin. Refrigerate until firm. Ice if wished. Cut into squares.

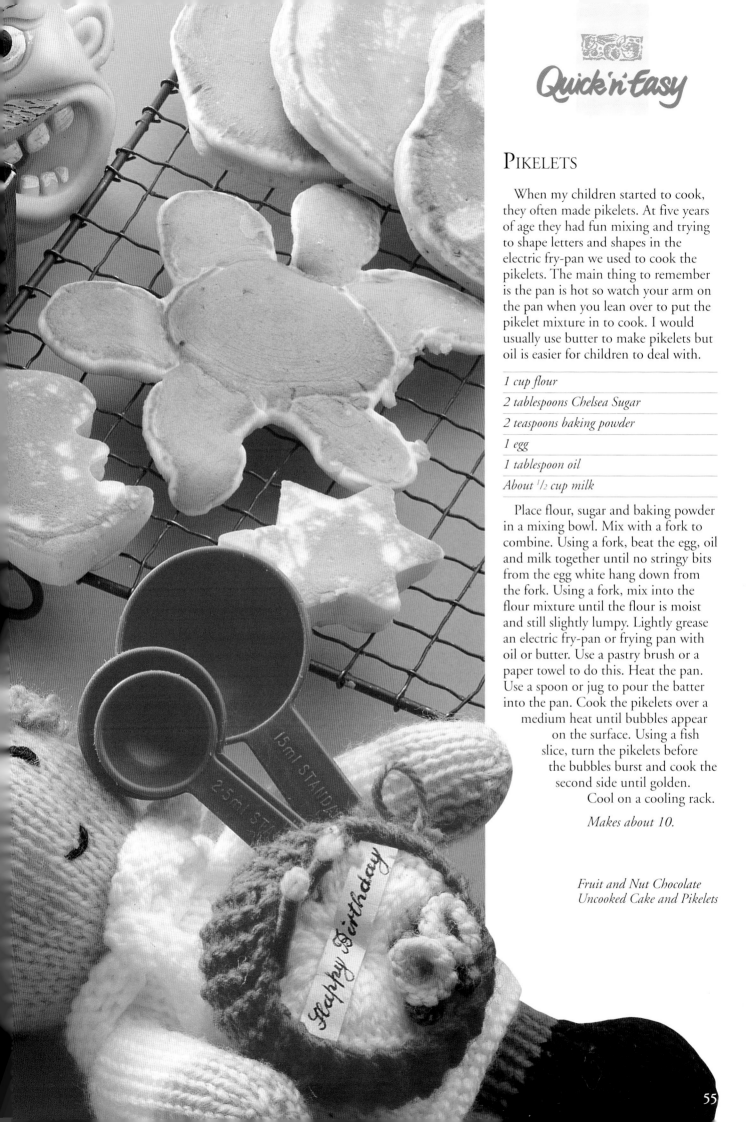

PIKELETS

When my children started to cook, they often made pikelets. At five years of age they had fun mixing and trying to shape letters and shapes in the electric fry-pan we used to cook the pikelets. The main thing to remember is the pan is hot so watch your arm on the pan when you lean over to put the pikelet mixture in to cook. I would usually use butter to make pikelets but oil is easier for children to deal with.

1 cup flour

2 tablespoons Chelsea Sugar

2 teaspoons baking powder

1 egg

1 tablespoon oil

About ¹/₂ cup milk

Place flour, sugar and baking powder in a mixing bowl. Mix with a fork to combine. Using a fork, beat the egg, oil and milk together until no stringy bits from the egg white hang down from the fork. Using a fork, mix into the flour mixture until the flour is moist and still slightly lumpy. Lightly grease an electric fry-pan or frying pan with oil or butter. Use a pastry brush or a paper towel to do this. Heat the pan. Use a spoon or jug to pour the batter into the pan. Cook the pikelets over a medium heat until bubbles appear on the surface. Using a fish slice, turn the pikelets before the bubbles burst and cook the second side until golden. Cool on a cooling rack.

Makes about 10.

Fruit and Nut Chocolate Uncooked Cake and Pikelets

Quick 'n' Easy

SCONES

Remember to wash your hands then turn the oven on before you start to make these scones.

2 cups flour
4 teaspoons baking powder
2 tablespoons Chelsea Sugar
50g butter
³/₄ cup milk

Sift flour and baking powder into a bowl. Mix in sugar. Using your finger-tips, rub the butter into the flour by gently rubbing the butter and flour together. When the butter has been rubbed in enough, the flour should look like coarse breadcrumbs. Add the milk to the flour mixture and quickly mix until the ingredients are all mixed together. Use your hands to press the dough together. Lightly dust a board or the kitchen bench with flour. Turn the dough onto this. Use your hands to gently press the dough to a square that is 3cm high. Cut the dough into squares. Place on an oven tray. Bake at 220°C for 10 to 15 minutes or until the scones look golden. Wrap the scones in a clean teatowel and leave to cool on a cooling rack.

Makes 6.

OTHER IDEAS FOR YUMMY SCONES

DATE SCONES - Add ¹/₂ cup chopped dates to the flour mixture after you have rubbed in the butter.

CHEESE SCONES - Leave the sugar out of the scones. Sprinkle grated cheese over the top of each scone. Take care not to get any cheese on the oven tray as it will burn.

DEVONSHIRE SCONES - Cut plain scones in half. Spread with raspberry jam and top with whipped cream that has been coloured with a few drops of red food colouring.

WHOLEMEAL SCONES

Scones were the first things I learnt to cook. They are a good way to start learning to cook. Remember to wash your hands and turn the oven on before you start cooking.

1 cup flour
1 cup wholemeal flour
4 teaspoons baking powder
2 tablespoons Chelsea Soft Brown Sugar
50g butter
³/₄ cup milk

Mix flour, wholemeal flour, baking powder and brown sugar together in a bowl. Using your finger tips, rub the butter into the flour by gently rubbing the butter and flour together. When the butter has been rubbed in enough, the flour should look like coarse breadcrumbs. Add the milk to the flour mixture and quickly mix until the ingredients are all mixed together. Use your hands to press the dough together. Lightly dust a board or the kitchen bench with flour. Turn the dough onto this. Use your hands to gently press the dough to a square that is 3cm high. Cut the dough into squares. Place on an oven tray. Bake at 220°C for 10 to 15 minutes or until the scones look golden. Wrap the scones in a clean teatowel and leave to cool on a cooling rack.

Makes 6.

Wholemeal Scones (left), Scones, Devonshire Scones and Shortenin' Bread

Quick'n'Easy

SHORTENIN' BREAD

Don't forget to turn the oven on before you start.

Flour

400g packet sweet short pastry

Chelsea Icing Sugar

Lightly dust a board or the kitchen bench with flour. Take the pastry from the packet and use a rolling pin or a bottle to roll the pastry out to 3mm thickness. When rolling pastry do not press hard. Roll gently away from you. Use a cutter to cut shapes from the pastry. Place shapes on an oven tray. Press left-over pastry together and re-roll. Cut out more shapes. Bake at 190°C for 7 to 10 minutes or until lightly golden. Take biscuits from the oven. Cool on a cooling rack. Dust with icing sugar by putting a teaspoon of icing sugar in a small sieve and sprinkling over the biscuits.

OTHER IDEAS FOR SHORTENIN' BREAD

Mix a $1/2$ teaspoon of cocoa or cinnamon with the icing sugar before sprinkling over the biscuits. Ice and decorate with hundreds and thousands.

ICING

1 cup Chelsea Icing Sugar

2 tablespoons hot water

Sift icing sugar into a bowl. Mix in enough hot water to make a smooth icing that is able to be spread.

Quick 'n' Easy

DESSERTS

*As my children grow up we seem to be permanently in a hollow
leg mode. That usually means they don't feel satisfied at the end
of their main course unless they have something sweet to finish.
The best solution is a quick dessert which is often based on fresh
fruit. It doesn't mean reaching for high fat ice-cream, especially
at a time when we should be trying to cut down our
fat consumption.
Here are a few recipes I have found useful standbys for lots of
occasions when a dessert is required in a hurry.
They are especially good for the winter when appetites have an
edge to them and can certainly be served with no trouble
when entertaining.*

QUICK APPLE SLAB

This is a great standby, especially for winter meals when appetites have an edge on them. I make this regularly for my family and it is always enjoyed. Leave the cloves out if you want; it still tastes great. Any leftovers are always enjoyed in a packed lunch. The 100% Apple used in this recipe is solid pack apple slices.

2 sheets pre-rolled flaky pastry

2 x 410g cans 100% Apple

¹/₂ teaspoon ground cloves

2 tablespoons Chelsea Raw Sugar

Place one pastry sheet on a baking tray. Pile apple on the pastry to within 1cm of the edge. Sprinkle cloves over. Brush pastry edge with water. Fold second pastry sheet in half and cut slashes at 1cm intervals to within 2cm of edges. Place pastry on top of apple. Press edges together. Sprinkle raw sugar over. Bake at 200°C for 15 to 20 minutes or until pastry is golden. To serve, cut into squares or rectangles. Serve with cream or custard.

Serves 4 to 6.

FRUIT WHIZZY

410g can 100% Apple or Apricot

¹/₄ cup custard powder

¹/₄ cup Chelsea Sugar

3 eggs

1¹/₂ cups milk

1 tablespoon Chelsea Icing Sugar

1 teaspoon ground cinnamon

Place apples or apricots, custard powder, sugar, eggs and milk in a food processor or blender. Process or blend until combined. Pour into a greased 4 cup capacity ovenproof dish. Bake at 190°C for 30 minutes or until set. Mix icing sugar and cinnamon together. Dust over surface of fruit whizzy.

Serves 4 to 6.

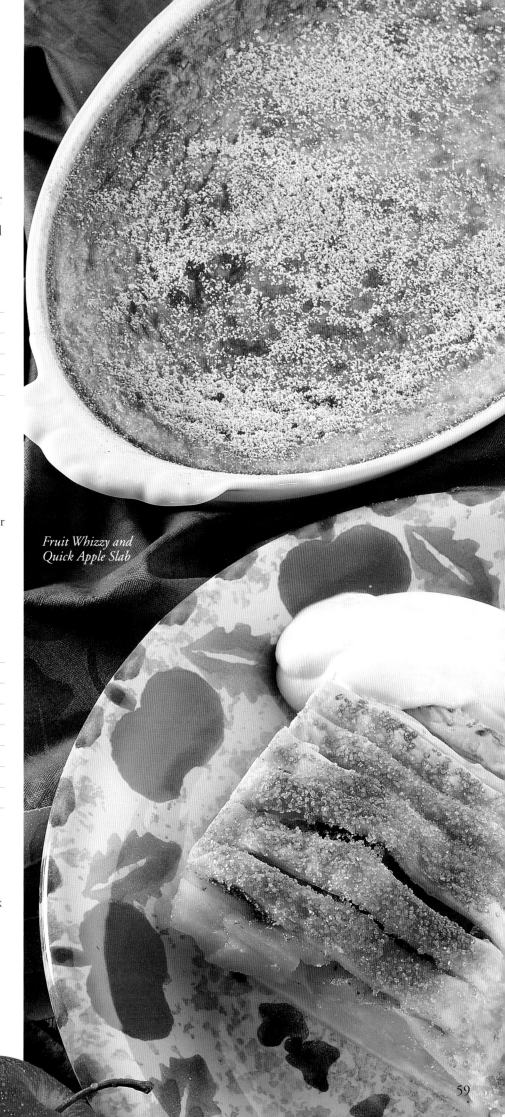

Fruit Whizzy and Quick Apple Slab

Quick 'n' Easy

IMPOSSIBLE COCONUT PIE

There are many sweet and savoury versions of this pie. It's quick to mix but takes a little longer to cook than many desserts so a little planning is required if you need dessert in a hurry. If you don't have a food processor or blender, make sure the butter is soft and use a rotary beater. Mix the coconut in at the end.

3 eggs
50g butter
1/2 cup flour
1 1/2 cups milk
3/4 cup Chelsea Sugar
1 cup coconut
1 teaspoon grated orange rind

Place eggs, butter, flour, milk, sugar, coconut and orange rind in the bowl of a food processor or blender. Process or blend until combined. Pour into a greased 20cm quiche dish or pie plate. Bake at 180°C for about 50 minutes or until the pie springs back when lightly touched.

Serves 4 to 6.

PAVLOVA ROLL

Use any fresh seasonal fruit to fill this roll.

4 egg whites
1 cup Chelsea Caster Sugar
1 cup cream
1/4 cup passionfruit pulp

Beat egg whites until stiff. Gradually add caster sugar and beat until stiff and glossy. Spread meringue into a baking paper-lined 20 x 30cm sponge roll tin. Bake at 180°C for 15 minutes or until golden and set. Turn meringue onto a piece of baking paper. Remove paper base. Leave to cool for 5 to 10 minutes. Beat cream until thick. Mix in passionfruit pulp. Spread over meringue. Roll meringue up from the long side, using the paper to help. Chill before serving.

Serves 6.

COTTAGE CLAFOUTI

250g pot cottage cheese

¹/₂ cup milk

3 eggs

¹/₂ cup Chelsea Sugar

¹/₂ cup flour

2 teaspoons grated lemon rind

50g butter

Chelsea Icing Sugar

Place cottage cheese, milk, eggs, sugar, flour, lemon rind and butter in the bowl of a food processor or blender. If there is too much mixture for the capacity of your appliance, leave the milk until the end and then mix in. Pour mixture into a greased 20cm quiche dish or flan tin. Bake at 180°C for 35 to 40 minutes or until set. Serve warm, dusted with sifted icing sugar.

Serves 6.

Impossible Coconut Pie,
Chocolate Delicious,
Cottage Clafouti
and Pavlova Roll

CHOCOLATE DELICIOUS

This is the ever-popular self-saucing pudding.

50g butter

1 cup flour

2 teaspoons baking powder

2 tablespoons cocoa

¹/₂ cup Chelsea Sugar

¹/₂ cup milk

1 teaspoon vanilla essence

¹/₂ cup Chelsea Soft Brown Sugar

1 tablespoon cocoa

1¹/₂ cups boiling water

Chelsea Icing Sugar

Melt butter in a saucepan large enough to mix all the ingredients. Sift flour, baking powder and first measure of cocoa into butter. Add sugar, milk and vanilla essence and beat with a wooden spoon until combined. Pour into a greased 4 cup ovenproof dish. Mix brown sugar and second measure of cocoa together. Sprinkle over batter in dish. Pour boiling water over the back of a spoon onto the surface of the pudding. Bake at 180°C for 35 to 40 minutes or until pudding springs back when lightly touched. Dust with sifted icing sugar.

Serves 4 to 6.

Quick 'n' Easy

APPLE CRUMBLE DESSERT CAKE

125g butter

1 cup Chelsea Sugar

2 eggs

³/₄ cup low fat milk

2 cups flour

4 teaspoons baking powder

TOPPING

2 Granny Smith apples

¹/₂ cup flour

2 tablespoons Chelsea Soft Brown Sugar

1 teaspoon baking powder

50g butter

Place butter and sugar in a saucepan large enough to mix all the ingredients. Heat, stirring, until butter melts. Beat eggs and milk together. Add egg mixture and sifted flour and baking powder to saucepan. Mix to combine. Pour into a baking paper-lined 20cm cake tin. Arrange apple slices over cake, pressing the thin edge into cake. Sprinkle topping over. Bake at 180°C for about 1 hour or until an inserted skewer comes out clean. Serve warm with softly whipped cream.

Serves 6 to 8.

TOPPING

Peel apples. Cut into quarters, core then cut each quarter into 4 slices. Mix flour, brown sugar and baking powder together. Rub in butter until mixture resembles coarse crumbs.

CAUGHT SHORT SUMMER DESSERT

When I'm asked to provide dessert for a function this is what I usually whisk up. It's always been well received, even by some of the world's most famous food writers. Vary the quantities for this depending on how many you have to serve. Try this at a summer barbecue.

400g packet sweet short pastry

Chelsea Icing Sugar

300ml cream

1 cup natural sweetened yoghurt

1kg fresh dessert fruit

Roll pastry out on a lightly floured board. Cut into hearts using a heart-shaped pastry cutter. Place on a lightly floured oven tray. Bake at 190°C for 7 to 10 minutes or until lightly golden. Cool on a cooling rack. Dust with sifted icing sugar. Whip cream until soft. Mix in yoghurt. Prepare fruit if necessary. Arrange on a platter. Arrange biscuits around fruit and serve with cream and yoghurt sauce.

Serves 8 to 10.

Caught Short Summer Dessert and Apple Crumble Dessert Cake

Quick 'n' Easy

INDEX